The Most Powerful People On Earth Revealed

Leonard MP Kayiwa

Unless otherwise indicated, all Scripture
quotations are taken from the
New King James version of the Bible,
and the old King James version

Formatted and typed by:
Pastor Gail B. Kayiwa, D.D.

Cover Design and Illustrations by:
Dr. Leonard Kayiwa
kayiwaministries@yahoo.com

The Most Powerful People on Earth Revealed
ISBN 978-0-9717609-3-6
Copyright ©2018 by Leonard MP Kayiwa

Leonard Kayiwa Ministries
P.O. Box 1898
Bolingbrook, Illinois 60440

GOD

LOVES

TO

EMPOWER

YOU

Golden Rule No. 2

God

Will take you

As far

As

You are willing

To

Go

"if you are willing and obedient, you shall eat the good of the land; But if you refuse and rebel, you shall be devoured by the sword", For the mouth of the Lord has spoken." Isaiah 1:19   nkjv Bible

Dedication

THIS BOOK IS DEDICATED
TO THE PEOPLE
IN
AFRICA, AMERICA
EUROPE, CHINA,
AUSTRALIA,
MIDDLE EAST, ETC.,
AND
TO ALL CHURCHES
AROUND THE WORLD
PLUS,
THOSE WHO HAVE WORKED
WITH ME
TO MAKE THE BOOK AVAILABLE
TO THE
NATIONS:
MY WIFE, DR. GAIL B. KAYIWA
AND MY CHILDREN
MOSES EMMANUEL KAYIWA
JOSHUA ISRAEL KAYIWA
ENOCH DEOGRACIOUS KAYIWA,
AND
MARY DEBORAH NAKAYIWA

ENDORSEMENTS

BISHOP LEONARD KAYIWA IS ONE OF THE MOST PROLIFIC WRITERS EVER KNOWN TO ME, HIS WRITINGS CARRY A VERY SPECIAL ANOINTING. JUST READING A BOOK LIKE THIS MAKES YOU REALIZE WHAT GOD ALREADY HAS FOR YOU. YOU END UP FEELING GREAT ABOUT YOURSELF, AND DESIRING TO DO MORE TO MAKE A DIFFERENCE ON EARTH. THIS BOOK, 'THE MOST POWERFUL PEOPLE ON EARTH REVEALED' IS A GIFT TO HUMANITY FROM THE LORD, GOD ALMIGHTY THROUGH HIS SERVANT, LEONARD KAYIWA. THE TRUTH HAS BEEN REVEALED ABOUT THE STATE OF HUMAN BEINGS AND WHAT MAKES ONE GREAT. THE DOOR IS WIDE OPEN FOR ANY TRUE SEEKER TO ENTER PEACEFULLY. GOD BLESS YOU ALL.

BISHOP TODD

Justice has been done. The Word has been properly divided; it is line upon line, precept upon precept, a little here and a little there, with testimonies to back it.

BROTHER SAM HONNOLD

DR. GAIL B. KAYIWA

God had done it again! It is amazing to see the hand of God that is upon my husband's life. Once again, Bishop Leonard Kayiwa has obeyed the voice of God, and put in writing, a very powerful book, from God Almighty, entitled: 'The Most Powerful People on Earth Revealed.' I promise you, it is a must read!! You will rejoice as you travel with him on this God approved trip into truth, love, peace and Godly counsel, regarding the most powerful people on earth. Don't be surprised if while you are on the journey reading this gem, that you find someone that you know quite well, yourself!!! I personally took the journey and found myself. Happy reading.!

DR. GAIL B. KAYIWA, B.A., M.A., PROFESSIONAL GRANT WRITER

mrsrev3@gmail.com

We thank God for Bishop Leonard Kayiwa. I really believe this is one of the most important books that has ever graced your path. Through this book, Dr. Leonard Kayiwa has moved me to look at life a little bit more closely, especially when he talked about the Rapture. I realized the uniqueness of a 'Believer' in the light of the scriptures. The man of God, with the simplicity of a child, has let us know that the 'Believers' matter, and that they have a very, very important role to play in our society. This book is a game changer, it resolves the identity crisis with solid, solid proofs of testimonies backed with scriptures of the experiences of real people. This writing makes a believer out of you. The layout of this book is magnificent, the illustrations are heavenly, through its pages, you literally see a clear picture concerning greatness; the greatness that is redemptive. Bishop Leonard Kayiwa is a blessing to humanity, we really thank God for calling this man of God and giving him the ability to flow in revelation knowledge, so that all of us can benefit. My prayer to the reader of this book; may the Lord God Almighty Reveal Himself to you more, through the pages of this book.

Brother James Huntington

I am a 'Born Again' Christian, this book is an "eye-opener", every Christian should have a copy of this book. This book is a tool for soul winning, when you read it, you get empowered to go out there and tell people about Jesus Christ. The man of God presented our Lord Jesus Christ, the Son of the Living God, to the whole world, in a very, very powerful way. Jesus Christ has been properly lifted up before the whole world in this book, and many are going to be drawn to Him. Our brother Leonard Kayiwa's love for Jesus Christ is on all the pages of this book, no wonder he is carrying a very powerful anointing. Many who read this book, are going to become very effective soul winners and purpose shall be the lead in whatever they do, for in this book, you clearly discover your purpose as a child of God. I have read the book, I feel energized, greatly motivated, empowered to reach out to the people with the love of God. My attitude has been greatly changed, I operate more in compassion these days knowing who I am on earth. God sent Bishop Leonard Kayiwa to us with good news. Read this book, recommend it to the whole world, for they need it, for such a time as this. Your brother in Christ,

John Carrington

This book is a 'pearl' of great price, this is a gem in your hands. It is a treasure very rare to find, and now in your possession. What amazes me is the fact that English is not the first language of the author, but the way words are chosen in this book, is so royal that you can't help but realize that this is a God sent message, through a vessel that is willing to be used by God. Truth is in this book, backed with very lively testimonies, that when you are reading the book, you feel heavenly empowered. Get the book!!!

Sarah Deborah Jeremiah, MD

BOOKS HAVE BEEN WRITTEN REGARDING VARIOUS TOPICS, BUT THIS BOOK IS VERY, VERY UNIQUE. ANYBODY WHO GETS POSSESSION OF THIS BOOK CAN'T HELP BUT CHANGE TO THE BETTER. THIS BOOK DRAWS GREATNESS OUT OF A HUMAN BEING. THROUGH IT, YOU GET GROUNDED AND RECONNECTED IN GOD. FOR MANY WHO HAVE BEEN SEEKING FOR SOMETHING MORE, THROUGH THIS BOOK, YOU COME IN GRIPS WITH IT – THAT IS JESUS CHRIST.

ANY SINCERE SEEKER OF THE TRUTH, YOU HAVE A GUIDE IN YOUR HANDS, AND THIS GUIDE IS TRUTHFUL. THE AUTHOR, BISHOP LEONARD KAYIWA, HAS PRESENTED THE TRUTH ABOUT, 'THE MOST POWERFUL PEOPLE ON EARTH' WITHOUT ANY PARTIALITY. THE EVALUATION IS AMAZING, IT IS LIKE THE HUMAN RACE HAS BEEN PUT UNDER A BIG MAGNIFYING GLASS, AND FOUND IN NEED OF A SAVIOR. A SOLUTION HAS BEEN PRESENTED TO THE WHOLE WORLD BY THIS RENOWN AUTHOR, DR. LEONARD KAYIWA, WHOSE STYLE OF WRITING IS EXTREMELY UNIQUE.

Brother/Professor Charles, PhD

ORAL ROBERTS UNIVERSITY, HARVARD UNIVERSITY, PRINCETON UNIVERSITY

FORWARD

IT IS GOD'S WILL FOR YOU TO BE HONORED

The Bible says, in the Book of Jeremiah Chapter Thirty-Three, verse three, "Call to Me, and I will answer you, and show you great and mighty things, which you do not know." Jer 33:3

God is love; God is omnipotent; God is omniscient; and omnipresent. He is right where you are and loves bringing greatness to you.

God Almighty bids us, that is all of us; regardless of our background, nationality, status in the community, religion, etc. to call upon Him: that is to seek Him, to come in His presence, to search out for Him.

Then He promises that when we come in His presence, He will answer us regarding anything of concern to us.

What makes this call so powerful, is the fact that He promises to show us great and mighty things which we know not.

Many people are where they are in their belief, not because they necessarily love to be on that platform, but only that they found themselves among people who believed that way: God knows that. That is why He gives every human being a chance to know the truth.

The purpose of the Ministry of the Written Word, is to make available the Word of God to people like you and me who are hungry for God. For the Bible says, "Blessed are those who hunger and thirst for righteousness, For they shall be filled". Matt 5:8

One of the big challenges we have in our society today on the earth, is identity, many understand that what you are connected to could determine your identity. If you are connected to something weak, possibly you may reflect that. If you are connected to something very, very powerful, maybe that is what you will become.

In this book, you will find what you are supposed to be connected to.

Your Brother in Christ,

Bishop Leonard Kayiwa, D.D.

DR. BISHOP LEONARD MP KAYIWA

ABOUT THE AUTHOR

Dr. Leonard Kayiwa is a highly anointed servant of God, he started ministering before the Lord, early in life. An altar boy at nine years old, he served at St. Peter's Cathedral at Nsambya, Kampala, Uganda, Africa. He would serve in every mass, almost every day.

His love for God began early. After finishing primary school at St. Peter's Primary, he joined St. Henry's College Kitovu, Masaka, Uganda, where God blessed him with very high marks in school, whereby he could devote a lot of his time helping his fellow students in whatever subject they needed help in. God gifted him, especially in mathematics, physics, chemistry, history, technical drawing and Biblical studies.

He joined Makerere University in Kampala, Uganda where "he got born again", which resulted in a drastic change in his life. He did Irrigation and Water Conservation Engineering at Hahai University in Nanjing, China and received the Baptism of the Holy Spirit with evidence of speaking in tongues in Hong Kong, at the new Covenant Church. God does unusual miracles through his life and many have become "born again" through his ministry.

TABLE OF CONTENTS

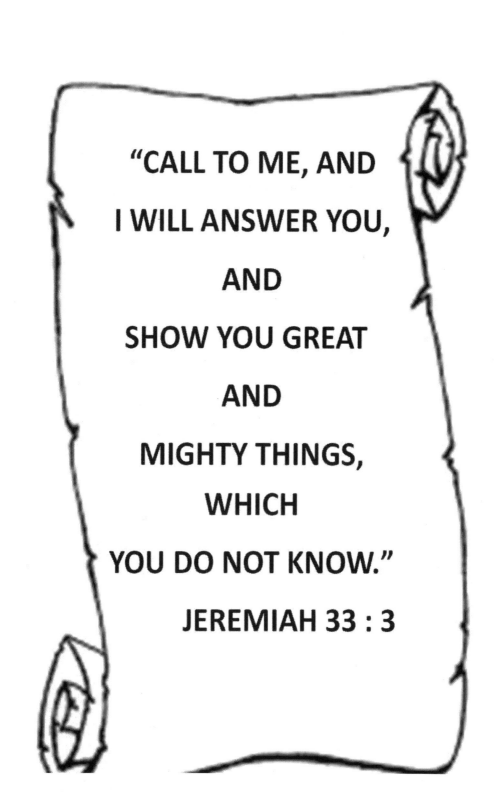

BUT TO YOU

WHO

Fear MY NAME

THE

SON OF RIGHTEOUSNESS

SHALL ARISE

WITH

HEALING

IN HIS WINGS;

AND

YOU SHALL GO OUT

AND

GROW FAT LIKE

STALL FED

CALVES

MALACHI 4:2

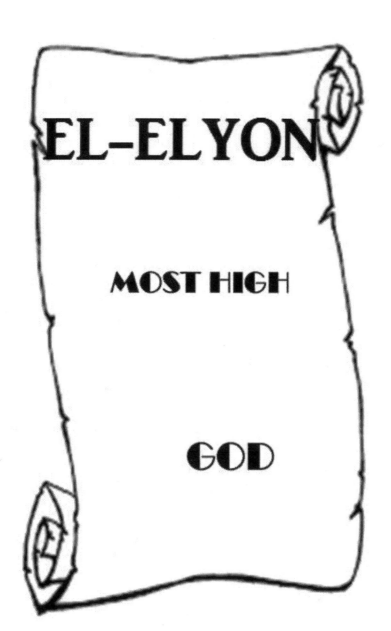

1

POWERFUL

"for the Word of God is living and powerful, and sharper than any two-edged sword, piercing even to the division of soul and spirit, and of joints and marrow, and is a discerner of the thoughts and intents of the heart. Heb 4:12

You have in your possession one of the most educative books ever to cross your path, and I believe it is by Divine providence.

There are different things that people consider when they hear the word 'powerful.' One of them is "embrace" and the other is "run." Different experiences in different circumstances have led to various definitions of that word. Today, let us look at it together in the right perspective.

How many looked at 'Powerful' during Idi Amin's Regime of Terror

I was about nine years old when Idi Amin took power through a coup in 1971. I had just begun my duties as

The Most Powerful People on Earth Revealed

An Altar Boy in a Catholic Church, that was near the school I attended, for my primary education. This level of education is referred to as elementary school in the U.S.A. This was at St. Peter's Primary School, in Nsambya, Kampala, Uganda, Africa. By that time, education was taken very seriously. Uganda had one of the most thriving universities in the world, Makerere University, and a lot of other wonderful colleges such as: St. Henry's College, Kitovu; St. Mary's College, Kisubi; Namilyango College, etc. In addition, there were a number of church attendees, and many took prayer as part of their life-style.

There were a number of different denominations: Catholic, Church of Uganda, Pentecostals (Evangelicals), Seventh Day Adventist, Orthodox Churches, and people of the Moslem religion. I was born in Mulago Hospital in Kampala, Uganda and most of my relatives as well as my parents lived in Kampala, Uganda, which is the seat of power and the capitol city of Uganda.

Insight into How We Were Brought Up

Many children, especially those under 18 years of age, we were instructed at school to value life, to do to others what we would want them to do to us. "Therefore, whatever you want men to do to you, do also to them, for this is the Law and the Prophets." Matt 7:12 What we were told was very much in line with Jesus's teaching on the mountain in the Gospel of Matthew.

Blessed are the merciful, For they shall obtain mercy. Blessed are the pure in heart, For they shall see God. Blessed are the peacemakers, For they shall be called the sons of God. Blessed are those who are persecuted for righteous ness sake, for theirs is the kingdom of heaven. Blessed are you when they revile and persecute you, and say all kinds of evil against you falsely for My sake. "Rejoice and be exceedingly glad, for great is your reward in heaven, for so they persecuted the prophets

who were before you. "You are the salt of the earth but if salt loses its flavor, how shall it ..." Matt 5:7-13

Most children of different faiths, especially Christians, took on those instructions and tried their best to live by that Code of Conduct. We respected our elders and we gave them our ears, expecting to receive some wisdom and guidance on how to live. We kind of thought that education, and instructions of that day were very valuable; and that 'powerful' was to adhere by values that add dignity to society.

A Military Coup: 'Dictator Idi Amin Ushered In.'

I was on my way to school and our school was next to the police barracks, which also housed the Milton Obote Special Forces. Those were the men and women who were supposed to be very loyal to the Regime and president at that time – Milton Obote. When suddenly the entire area was engulfed in ear deafening noise of military tanks firing, gun fire and grenade explosions.

That day school was interrupted! we all ran to different hiding places. Astounded and amazed, wondering what that could be. This lasted nearly seven hours that day. Some people were saying something 'powerful' is happening, really? Well, we needed to know the truth, for the truth sets free. Jesus said in the

Gospel of John, "And you shall know the truth, and the truth shall make you free." John 8:32 Everyone was anxious to know what all the sound of gunfire represented; what had happened, and what it meant to the world, as well as to the nation of Uganda.

You might be saying, Bishop Kayiwa, why should we look into such events now. Are they really relevant; since we are analyzing the word 'powerful'? Yes, all this is relevant for us to be able to fairly give meaning to the word 'powerful'. This is part of the central theme of this book.

Some people take to the streets celebrating the military Coup.

Not many days after the coup, which brought Idi Amin and his henchmen to power; about two days into the regime, many people were busy outside dancing, singing and celebrating the regime change, claiming that something very extraordinarily good was happening to Uganda and the world at large.

Many had been murdered by Idi Amin and his soldiers, in the process of grabbing power. The gun fire that we heard on the day of the coup, as well as the days that followed, had left many of my fellow students parentless and injured. Buildings had been shelled down. Soldiers were everywhere with guns, hunting for those they considered to be their foes. Dead bodies were on the streets and a large number of homes were ransacked and looted by some of those celebrators who claimed that something 'powerful' had happened.

I could sense as a child that my parents were not comfortable with what had happened. I could hear them talking about 'wickedness' ushered in; disguised as 'powerful'. They did not believe that the new regime was going to bring decency to people's lives, for to any reasonable person, 'red flags' were everywhere.

The Dictatorship Claims of 'Powerful'

These men and women quickly claimed to be the most powerful people in the world!! And demanded absolute loyalty. Idi Amin and his fellow thugs quickly shut down the Parliament and put aside the Constitution of the nation of Uganda. We ended up with a situation like that which took place at the conception of the United States of America, 'taxation without representation'. The dictatorship abolished freedom of speech.   Anyone who had a different opinion, contrary to theirs was deemed to be an enemy.   These people were not peaceable and had zero tolerance for descent. You just either let them have their way, or you get killed.   As a child growing up, I was perplexed by the behavior of these adults.   I wondered whether all that we were taught in school, as well as at home, meant anything to them.   They seemed to operate in fear.

These rulers were completely opposite of what I believe in as a "born again" believer now.   The scripture in the book of Second Timothy, "For God has not given us a spirit of fear, but of power and of love and of a sound mind." 2 Tim 1:7, throws a lot of light on their demeanor.   These soldiers were full of fear, but disguised themselves as 'powerful.'

In this book, God has sent me to let you know, the most powerful people on earth.   It is very important that you come to glimpse with reality because for you to perceive this revelation properly, I have to take you through real life events.   We have to have some knowledge.   For the Bible says, "My people are destroyed for lack of knowledge.   Because you have rejected knowledge, I also will reject you from being

Priest for Me; Because you have forgotten the law of your God, I also will forget your children." Hos 4:6 We are all God's people, created by the Lord God Almighty, and every human being whether in; Uganda, Kenya, China, Russia, the United States of America, Chile, Cameroon, Argentina, Togo, Tanzania, Britain, Mexico, Vietnam, Nigeria, South Africa, Australia, Canada, Rwanda...etc. We were made in the image of God. As it is written, "Then God said, "Let Us make man in Our image, according to Our likeness; let them have dominion over the fish of the sea, over the birds of the air, and over the cattle, over all the earth and over every creeping thing that creeps on the earth. " Gen 1:26

Many of my childhood friends, who attended elementary school with me at St. Peter's Primary School, Nsambya, lost at least one of their parents in very mysterious circumstances. People would go to work and never come back home again. Truly this was not 'powerful' but wickedness. Those Idi Amin regime people were very cunning. They disguised as if they were for the people, while actually, they were the opposite. The wisdom they operated in was demonic, sensual, and not from above, though they boasted of being very wise. "Who is wise and understanding among you? Let him show by good conduct that his works are done in the meekness of wisdom. But if you have bitter envy and self-seeking in your hearts, do not boast and lie against the truth. This wisdom does not descend from above, but is earthly, sensual, demonic. For where envy and self-seeking exist, confusion and every evil thing are there." Jam 3:13-16

They had guns, artilleries, grenades, tanks, war planes, swords, armored vehicles, rocket propellers... etc. and the laws were such that the civilians could not possess weapons. They took the tax money collected from the same people under the regime and used it to subject the civilians to inconceivable torture. They made sure that many believe that they are 'powerful' and unmovable. There was so much misleading propaganda put out there on T.V. and radio, as well as in newspapers, even songs were manipulated so that most of the music was about praising the dictator and his regime. The only comparison to that extremism would be the fascist regime of Hitler in Germany, that caused a lot of bloodshed. In fact, Idi Amin declared himself to be a 'life president'!! One to rule Uganda all the days of his life. In addition, he claimed to be God

Sent and one of his goals was to turn Uganda into an Islamic nation, which never happened. As I write this book, Uganda has so many Christian, as well as people of different faiths, because of the existing freedom of worship. Something else, which was very confusing, was the dictator's claim that he feared no man except God, although he and his henchmen were busy killing a lot of God's people.

This is how on the news everyday they had to introduce, as well as proclaim his presidency, to the people: -

'One to rule the Republic of Uganda all the days of his life, AL haji, General, Field Marshall, Conquer of the British Empire, One Decorated with a Military Cross, and the Victory Cross, Dr. Idi Amin Dadda'

I really believe that the reason why he demanded all this praise, was because he knew that inside him was an emptiness that desperately needed to be filled.

Evangelical Churches Are Abolished in Uganda

The dictatorship and its proprietors of wickedness suddenly abolished all non-denominational churches in Uganda. These were churches that believed in evangelism, in the miraculous power of God. They were also people of prayer and sure enough they carried themselves around with dignity, confessing that they are born again, as well as Bible believers.

For some reason, the dictator and his henchmen, though they portrayed themselves as the most powerful people on earth, having the power to terminate anybody's life at their pleasure, yet they seemed to dread the 'born again people as well as being afraid of their prayers. Soldiers would be sent to church gatherings to intimidate as well as throw people of God in jail. Their acts were really deceptive. "The wicked man does deceptive work, But he who sows righteousness will have a sure reward." Prov11: 18 The whole regime was very wicked.

Many wondered why, of all churches, the dictatorship was going violently after people who were not at all armed with guns, swords, and explosives. What these believers had were Bibles, praise, worship, and prayers. In the natural, it was like an elephant being afraid of an ant.

The news of the shutting down of the evangelical churches, was considered by many who belonged to other large religious groups as insignificant, and some received it with joy! None of them voiced their disagreement with that inappropriate decision. Some even rejoiced about it, for people were becoming 'born again' believers, and leaving some of those religions to join the Evangelicals.

I was not yet a born again Christian then. I was Catholic and an Altar Boy at St. Peter's Cathedral, Nsambya, Kampala, Uganda. We had just seen a Nun, missionary from Italy, shot at the parish by an unknown gunman. She was shot in the leg. She lay right there on the ground, wallowing in her blood. She was shot as she came out of her car to go to her office. That terrifying scene never left my memory. We were at the primary school grounds when this happened. Many students saw the horrifying event from a distance.

The dictatorship continued to go after Catholic priests, killing some of them. They went also after the Ugandan Anglican Church priests picking them up from pulpits, as they conducted church services, and taking them to unknown destinations for torture, and eventually killing them. We witnessed all of this, it was a time of much uncertainty and injustice of the highest level. The dictatorship claimed to be 'powerful' as well as untouchable, calling good evil and evil good. "Woe to those who call evil good, and good evil; Who put darkness for light, and light for darkness; Who put bitter for sweet, and sweet for bitter!" Is 5:20

Idi Amin was of the Moslem religion, and many Moslems supported him. Though everybody had to pay taxes to keep the government going, the people he put in most governmental positions and offices were either from his tribe or of the Moslem religion; it was even so, with the military. These people took most of the jobs. They were over the police, prison, education, revenue system, businesses, and foreign affairs. He made governors, mayors, and government ministers out of his place of birth, as well as some from Sudan. This regime did not reflect the make-up of the nation of Uganda. It was all sect eristic and very burdensome to the taxpayers. This is what many people called 'powerful'!

False 'Powerful'

I was at St. Henry's College, Kitovu, in the City of Masaka, Uganda, when it became very clear to me that this regime; dictatorship, was not really 'powerful.' The teachers were not properly paid and the schools were not cared for as they ought to have been. We were never fed properly any more at school, for the government money was mostly spent on buying weapons of war; military assets, as well as on the regime sustainers, who were getting a lion's share of the cake-the tax payer's money and money from coffee, and mineral resources. Ingenuity was suppressed, these people could not tolerate an innovative society or wise people. The dictatorship was an enemy of education, so the pillars of education of our society; school, family, place of employment, places of worship, and hospitals, were under siege, propelled by ignorance. Buildings were dilapidated, a proof that they had a false 'powerful' description of themselves. What they claimed to be powerful, was truly wickedness. This confirms the words of our Lord Jesus Christ in the book of John chapter ten, "The thief does not come except to steal, and to kill, and to destroy. I have come that they may have life, and that they may have it more abundantly." John 10:10

'Power' That Comes to Steal, Kill and Destroy Is Not 'Powerful'

I have used the circumstances I lived through to analyze 'Powerful,' by practically walking you through the time of adversity, we experienced growing up in a filthy dictatorship from 1971 to 1979; a regime that operated in defiance of all the values that were presented to us as children growing up. These people within the nation of Uganda, chose to be parasites and a destruction to every positive attribute of life. Just as Hitler and his henchmen were killers, so were these.

I believe you are now agreeing with me, that stealing peoples' property at gun point, taking away justice from the people, attacking the judicial system, and using military courts to settle civilian disputes is not healthy at all. Killing people on suspicion that they may not be your fans, and stealing their properties is absolutely no 'powerful.' It is wickedness.

Destroying dreams that God put in people's lives does not advance progress nor ingenuity. The results of that is not a powerful nation, but a weak one. This is exactly what happened at that time to the nation Uganda in East Africa between 1971 and 1979. I lived through this, we experienced it, many witnessed the pain which the people went through. The tears shed by families who were torn apart and the unspeakable destruction. We as kids used to wonder what had gone wrong with those particular adults, who had no sense at all and behaved as demons.

The Ground was not Levelled for Everybody to Bare Arms

The people of the Idi Amin dictatorship were not really what they claimed to be. The regime was afraid of the people, the recruiting into the military was such that the clansmen and immediate family of the dictator were put in all key military positions at the expense of the tax payers.

Most people recruited were those who spoke the language Amin spoke, who lived around that area of his birth. People of the Islam faith, this regime was more of a Moslem faith controlled community. Many had been told killing a Christian was alright to do, because they are infidels – nonbelievers.

The dictatorship disguising itself to be 'powerful' was making sure that people do not join the army on equal terms, for they knew that the only way they lorded over others was through depriving them of their weapons of defense. Deep in themselves they lacked confidence, peace, internal security and confidence.

Many of us were never trained to handle guns. Our neighbors, like Tanzania, trained its people how to use military equipment. No wonder when Idi Amin invaded the nation of Tanzania, his army was no match to them, for a regime that deprives its people of knowledge, lacks wisdom, and that is not 'powerful.'

One advancing by suppressing others is not 'powerful'. We see a bit of this in the book of Exodus in the Bible, after Joseph had passed away in Egypt. God had used Joseph to bring prosperity to Egypt. Joseph was sold to Egypt and brought into that empire as a slave. He was supposed to work for his slave masters for pennies. Normally, slave masters cheat and deprive their subjects of their God given rights. Slavery is economic exploitation and abuse of that which was created in the image of God, and always faces the severe judgements of God, anywhere it is practiced.

Slave Master's Depravity, in the Book of Exodus in the Holy Bible

The slave masters want to give an impression to their subjects that they are 'powerful.' Though, deep in their hearts (conscious), they know that the reason why they exercise slavery is to take advantage of what others do not know. In order to keep them bound, they have to deprive them of their fair pay, education, and right to vote.

The slave masters have to keep their subjects away from education, for if you educate a person, soon they will find out that all men are created equal and basically have similar aspirations and goals. They also have to take away from them the right to bear arms, because they understand that if they get "gun power," that would be the end of the bondage.

You can concur with me in this by looking into the China Revolution, whereby the people took power away from the few who claimed to be 'powerful.' You also witness this in the Russian Revolution. I don't mean this revolution was perfect, but it seems those who were designated as subjects to injustice and atrocities of those who claimed to be 'powerful' eventually took 'power' and literally destroyed those regimes. Well, what happened to these so called 'powerful'? Maybe they were not powerful, but wicked.

Enslaving people is not powerful, but wickedness. It is an act that reveals weakness in the perpetrator's life.

Wickedness, not 'powerful,' cited in the story of Exodus 1:8

"Now there arose a new king over Egypt, who did not know Joseph." Ex 1:8 Joseph brought Egypt out of a very dangerous famine through revelation knowledge from God. Egypt survived the famine through the grace of God revealed in a man that was enslaved in Egypt.

The Bible continues to say, 'And he said to his people, *"Look, the people of the children of Israel are more and mightier than we; "come, let us deal shrewdly with them, lest they multiply, and it happen, in the event of war, that they also join our enemies and fight against us, and so go up out of the land."* Ex 1:9-10 This scripture in this Bible story clearly enables us to look into the mind of the oppressor; the thief, killer and destroyer of good.

We notice in this quotation that, the dictator – the king, had a group of people that he confided in. These were his like-minded conspirators and promoters of evil.

A Few Things to Look At:

I. The oppressor – slave master, knew; that might,

can be in anyone or a group irrespective of their origin.

> II. The king and his confidants knew that they were not really that 'powerful'. They had to use shrewdness in order to maintain dominance over those people.

Now, we can't go any further without looking at this word, 'shrewdness':

I began this book by introducing and sharing with you, historical facts I witnessed growing up in a shrewd regime. A regime that calls good, bad and evil good. A group of people with no moral code and disguising as 'powerful' while riding on other peoples sweat and hard labor. A military regime that added nothing decent to our economy, nor education, and really moved nothing forward, but to them ascendency was through pushing innovative people down. In other words, there were no forward achievements at all, except wielding guns, killing innocent people and destroying the pillars of civilization.

The word 'shrewdness' in this context, is a behavior by any one that presents a false face, appearance or action that basically through fraud, takes advantage of the other person's decency, goodness and generosity.

Powerful

This is when someone, or a people, claim untrue 'power,' which they actually do not possess, and they display themselves through evil conduct, cunningly, while hiding their true depravity.

The Sharp Difference in how Uganda and Tanzania Governed, between 1971 and 1972

When I was in China studying at their university, I met another international student from Tanzania, the neighboring country to Uganda and part of the East African community. He was a very brilliant student and was one of those who had obtained a full Chinese scholarship to advance in solar and biogas energy engineering. He informed me that in his country, students at a certain time had to go through some military training to learn how to handle weapons of war. He also told me he was one of those who fought to liberate the precious people of Uganda from the dictatorship of Idi Amin and his loyal soldiers.

Now, this was a very big contrast to us who grew up in Uganda. All the way from primary education up to the university, colleges, technical institutions, seminaries, and other institutions of learning. We were never given an opportunity to be exposed to military hardware. The ground was not leveled at all. These people of the infamous regime, between 1971 and 1972 shrewdly kept the knowledge of operating arms from the students at school. They knew that if we get to learn how to operate those arms, that would be the end of their oppression over us.

The first time I ever handled a gun, was when I was in China. The Chinese had a program whereby every one of their students, as well as international students, had to be trained in how to handle a firearm, as well as self-defense. It was part of military science.

I am a preacher of the Gospel of Jesus Christ, and God has called me to ministry. Then, I was a student studying Irrigation and Water Conservation Engineering in Nanjing, China. The Chinese people did equip me with the knowledge of how to operate weapons of warfare, but those dictators in Uganda who walked around portraying themselves as 'powerful' could not even allow us to come near weapons. They were just full of themselves, and full of fear, while on the outside, they were running around like a roaring lion seeking for somebody to devour, "Be sober, be vigilant; because your adversary the devil walks about like a roaring lion, seeking whom he may devour. Resist him, steadfast in faith, knowing that the same sufferings are experienced by your brotherhood in the world." I Pet 5:8-9. Well that is not how 'powerful' looks like! Those Amin soldiers were like an inflated balloon, which could easily be gotten rid of by a simple pin pierce.

The People Get Rid of the Notorious Regime of Idi Amin and its Shrewdness

Many Ugandans crossed over to Tanzania between 1971 and 1979. They ran for their lives. While there, they were trained to bear arms, which was a nightmare to the trickery of the dictatorship. With the help of Comrade Muwalimu Julius Nyerere, the then president of the United Republic of Tanzania, and Commander in Chief of the military, a man who believed in educating his people about science, they were able to overthrow the dictatorship in Uganda. They were completely defeated. We all witnessed that they were not at all, 'powerful' as they shrewdly claimed to be. They were just supremacists, extremists, murderers, destroyers and thieves and propagators of hate.

Let me present a number of important points here:

1) SUPREMISM IS NOT 'POWERFUL'.

2) EXTREMISM IS NOT 'POWERFUL'.

3) TORTURE IS NOT 'POWERFUL'.

4) WITCHCRAFT IS NOT 'POWERFUL'.

5) SORCERY IS NOT 'POWERFUL'.

6) BIGOTRY IS NOT 'POWERFUL'.

7) DICTATORSHIP IS NOT 'POWERFUL'.

8) BULLYING PEOPLE IS NOT 'POWERFUL'.

9) FALSE ACCUSATIONS ARE NOT 'POWERFUL'.

10) SECTARIANISM IS NOT 'POWERFUL'.

11) SOWING DISCORD AMONG PEOPLE IS NOT 'POWERFUL'.

12) DIVISIVE RHETORIC IS NOT 'POWERFUL'.

13) HATE IS NOT 'POWERFUL'.

14) KILLING PEOPLE WITH CHEMICAL WEAPONS IS NOT 'POWERFUL'.

15) ABORTING CHILDREN IS NOT 'POWERFUL'

Powerful

The war raged, some killed and others got killed. Many of the dictatorship soldiers became scattered everywhere. They seemed confused and helpless. There were also foreign troops fighting along with them; especially those from Libya, and other countries, who fell with the sword.

Bodies of Amin Soldiers Litter the Streets and Fields

The path to defeat and total damnation is wickedness. I saw the bodies of the soldiers of the Idi Amin dictatorship rotting all over the place and their weapons of destruction lying beside them. Decomposing bodies littered the streets and grounds; very terrifying scene to behold. I was about 17 years of age. We saw parts of fighter planes that were shot down, lying on the grounds of war. These were Russian made planes. Body parts of the riders were hanging on the trees. It was a very bad situation for dictatorship soldiers.

In my family, we owned a ranch. It was five square miles of farmland, in a place called Mawogola, near the town of Ssembabule in Uganda.

It was designated as-Ngabonzira Ranches. We were at the ranch when the final war in 1979 that deposed the dictator, Idi Amin and his regime was raging.

The Comparable Likeness of this War

This book is extremely important, especially in the time where people are trying to find identity. They are trying to figure out who they are, and what are their true roots, for everybody wants assurance that they are somebody. I want to let you know that you are somebody! That is why Jesus died for you on the cross. This book, 'The Most Powerful People on Earth Revealed,' is a pathway to your true identity. No wonder God is moving me to paint the picture of 'powerful' to any curious seeker of greatness.

The carnage that we witnessed in Uganda, Africa during the war that removed that infamous regime, between 1971 and 1979, its true comparison would be like the senseless civil war that was fought in the United States of America whereby the perpetrators of suffering seemed to act like demons, having no regard for life and liberty, including their own. They all raged with fierce fury and in the process, death overtook them. Their legacy was not 'powerful' nor great, but wickedness of course we applaud those who sacrificed to diffuse the situation, and many of them gave their ultimate sacrifice, others were maimed and disabled like what happened to many liberators from Tanzania.

The other comparison would be, the carnage that took place during the Adolf Hitler dictatorship, where his subjects were falsely misled that they were the most 'powerful' people on earth. As a result, they took it upon themselves to spread their mislead ideology through war and conquest. We all know, they lost. The truth is, they were not 'powerful' but wicked. We need to know the most powerful people on earth. Who are they? Continue reading.

The Soldiers of Idi Amin in their Depravity try to take our clothes off of us in order to escape death

We were at the cattle ranch in Mawogola that week, the ranch was almost forty miles from Masaka, one of the cities in Uganda. We were also about five miles from the nearby township, Ssembabule. The battle to remove the thugs and their presidency off the peaceful people of Uganda, was raging. The liberating army composed of Ugandans, Tanzanians, Chinese was gaining grounds over the dictatorship. The regime army had soldiers from Libya, as well as Sudan fighting alongside them.

These so called, 'powerful' soldiers of dictator Idi Amin had become very disparate, they were raping women, stealing money, destroying property and killing innocent civilians.

That week, they had placed a military tank on the hill near our ranch. This tank was firing nearly nonstop, for a solid week. The people of Tanzania and Uganda were able to shoot and destroy it. They had landed a long range missile on it, and it went in flames when struck by the liberating army's fire. The dictatorship had put a lot of resistance at that location, but eventually, their military assets were destroyed; the vehicles that they were traveling on were hit.

This made the soldiers very desperate, their nest was rattled by the 'Wakombozi' (a Swahili word for liberators).

The infamous Idi Amin, had spent a lot of the tax payer's money on buying war planes. The regime tried its best to use those planes to turn around the tide, but it did not work. The liberating army easily shot them down, using surface to air missiles.

This is how the liberating army from Tanzania conducted warfare; they never shot civilians, nor tortured the civilian population. Their target was the soldiers of the Idi Amin dictatorship, and the dictator in case they could catch him. They were after anybody in the regime's military uniform, and anybody pointing a gun or other weapons at them. These desperate soldiers resorted to undressing civilians at gun point; taking off their military uniform, and putting on the clothes they had forcefully seized from the people, to appear to be regular civilians, to escape the siege!

On that interesting day, I was at the ranch with a son to my father's sister – named Kizito. He was in his late 20's, maybe 27 years old. We were walking on the cow's trail, when we heard people shouting at us, commanding us to stop and stand still. Our ranch had bushes as well as clear grazing areas, hills and valleys, it was a very rich landscape. They were speaking in Swahili saying, 'simama' which means stop. I was about 17 years old. My cousin Kizito spoke to me and said, 'run, follow me into the bush!' We ran like deers, jumping over little ant hills and ponds, zig zagging, and made sure we never ran a straight route. We went right into the bush and came out on the other side. They shot two times at us, but they missed. We escaped being killed or being stripped of our clothes, and left naked and possibly being tortured.

I never was part of the first and second world war, but to us, the war that removed Idi Amin from power had that kind of magnitude. I understand the pain, hurt and carnage that extremists and supremacists like Hitler and his fellow thugs, inflicted on the human race, through the false propaganda of 'powerful.'

I would like to submit to you that that is not how you save people from whatever you claim to be the problem. The Bible says in the book of Romans, "for all have sinned and fall short of the glory of God, being justified freely by His grace through the redemption that is in Christ Jesus," Rom 3:23-24.

The depravity in man is due to a sinful nature, and until that is remedied man can claim 'power' which is not at all 'powerful,' but wickedness, which is evil, for wrong cannot resolve wrong. Continuing with the narrative in Exodus, Chapter One, verse ten; the regime of Pharaoh during that time, took pleasure in exploiting others. Their way of moving forward was to cunningly put their burdens on others. We see that in the 11th verse of that chapter. "Therefore they set taskmasters over them to afflict them with their burdens. And they built for Pharaoh supply cities, Pithom and Raamses. But the more they afflicted them, the more they multiplied and grew. And they were in dread of the children of Israel." Ex 1:11-12

Being in Dread

This group of thugs or people, were in dread of the children of Israel. That let us know, that Pharaoh and his soldiers were not really 'powerful' but just a bunch of hooligans, who used wickedness to kill, steal and destroy lives. Precious people of God, dread can be seen everywhere. In families, neighborhoods, schools, places of employment, on major city streets, in council meetings and government facilities, as well as in the market place.

Dread carries with it a state of being afraid of what they cannot conquer; a fear that leads one to act very unreasonably, for what they are dealing with is a deep knowing right in their conscious that whatever they are in dread of will never be favorable to them. In such circumstances, the ways human beings try to hide their fears, is by inventing wicked schemes. In the case of the Exodus story, Chapter 1, this dread filled people, started killing children. The Bible says, "Then the king of Egypt spoke to the Hebrew midwives, of whom the name of one was Shiphrah and the name of the other Puah; and he said, "When you do the duties of a midwife for the Hebrew women, and see them on the birthstools, if it is a son, then you shall kill him; but if it is a daughter, then she shall live." Ex 1:15-16.

Killing Children is not 'Powerful'

Killing babies in the womb of their mothers is not powerful

Subjecting Children to War is not 'Powerful' at All

This book is about the most powerful people on the earth, revealed. My task from God, is to bring you into an understanding of who these people are, 'the most powerful', and to do justice to this worldwide great topic. We had to analyze further, some of the terminologies used here, for what is unfolding right now before you, is a fundamental truth that will bring you to look at the world through the right lens.

Why This Subject is very Important

We are living in a time of identity crisis. People are

Powerful

researching their ancestry, others are joining sects and movements in order learn who they are and where they came from. Being a pastor, having an opportunity to hear from all kinds of people, it has dawned on me that many people want to be accepted and also want to feel great about themselves; bottom line, they want to be part of something 'powerful', which is fine.

I have had concerns like this from numerous people : -

Am I really powerful?

Do I matter?

Am I important?

What is important?

What is 'powerful'?

What is right?

Who am I?

What defines me?

How did I come to be who I am?

Are devils and demons real?

Does God exist? Who is really for me?

These questions have to be answered, so that there may be peace among nations, people, neighborhoods and in all areas of life.

As I conclude this chapter, I would like to bring to your attention Hebrews 4:12. "For the word of God is living and powerful, and sharper than any two-edged sword, piercing even to the division of soul and spirit, and of joints and marrow, and is a discerner of the thoughts and intents of the heart." What I assume that you that you and I are getting out of this passage is that there exists something called the 'word of God,' and according to the attributes assigned to it, it is classified as 'powerful'. This leads us to fairly conclude that where that word is, must be 'powerful.'

How We Looked at 'Powerful' in College

When I joined college in Uganda, it was during the Idi Amin regime and that was around 1976. In the city called Masaka, which was 83 miles from Kampala, the capital city of Uganda. The language I grew up speaking was Luganda; this is possibly the most widely spoken language in Uganda, it is very much used in day to day interaction. St. Henry's College had a motto;

"FOR GREATER HORIZONS,"

Powerful

We students in that place of learning, were expected to look further, search out more, fly higher and do our best. We were meant to be the cream of the crop. It was a boarding school which was started by Catholic Missionaries, on a very magnificent hill. It was a place of pride, with a number of dormitories and classroom buildings. At that time, the government of Uganda was in charge of such colleges monetarily, and for that reason, they were put under the oversight of the Ministry of Education. We had a uniform syllabus for all of those kinds of college, where we did the ordinary and the advanced level. Our college was on a very beautiful campus, and we were required to study there for six years before joining the university.

This college being a boarding school, led us to spending more time away from home, and just be in an academic environment. We were excited about our new place and environment: laboratories, art galleries, recreational rooms, chapels, agricultural gardens, ball fields, a very nice forest of ecliptic trees along the hill, theatres, and a lot of new ventures. It was really a time of exploits and much learning. We felt 'powerful'!!!

Is Knowledge 'Powerful?'

The subjects we studied then to begin with were: mathematics, biology, chemistry, physics, geography, technical drawing, history, accounting, literature, religious studies, English, agriculture, social studies, art and French. We were busy obtaining knowledge in order to make a difference in our lives and our surroundings. God says in the book of Hosea, Chapter Four, verse number six, "My people are destroyed for lack of knowledge, because you have rejected knowledge, I also will reject you from being priest for Me; Because you have forgotten the law of your God, I also will forget your children." Hos 4:6

Confusion Disguised as Knowledge

I have run into people who can't even tell the difference in colors. It concerns me because it pushes bad judgment on our children and consequently, confusion. I am talking about bad judgment driven by evil intent, which makes the toddlers wonder what is wrong with some adults. Being a student of Chemistry, and one who had to list physical and chemical properties of specimen, I learned to apply accuracy to my determinations. I don't just get up and call purple white; maroon black; pink yellow; brown black; chocolate black, pink white, or blue purple, for if we falsely identify specimen like that, then one can fairly say black is white, I don't believe that is sanely correct.

Powerful

What it really is, is insanity and worse, extremism. Most reasonable people agree that extremism of any form is not good. I was watching the news, and I saw a grieving mother of four children whose husband was killed by Isis, that is Moslem extremists. They came to her husband and insisted that he was not a true Moslem because he never grew a beard. The wife pleaded with the extremists and said, "My husband and I as well as our four young children, have been Moslem since birth, and we pray three times a day." But their assailants insisted that the man can't be a Moslem because he does not have a beard, and they violently cut off his head. Well, the mother of the four abandoned Islam for that, and turned to Jesus Christ as her Savior, with her four young children and had to leave that country and move to elsewhere, where people value life. Even though she had to go through a painful process as a refugee. Beloved, confusion disguised as knowledge is equal to wickedness. Know that cream is cream, white is white, black is black, purple is purple, pink is pink, green is green, every shade has a majesty created within it by God Almighty and it deserves its identity.

To tarry a little bit more on the thought above, being a person who speaks a number of languages, helps me to evaluate words very keenly, for words matter. I have studied Chinese and do speak it, I have studied English by God's grace, and do speak it, I have studied Luganda and do speak it, in fact, the first language that I spoke growing up, was Luganda in Uganda. Luganda is a very, very interesting language. It has amazing accuracy in the way it expresses things. In Luganda, one can describe a scene and all its contents, with laser sharp accuracy, so that when you look at it, you do not need to ask any questions. It is a very poetic language.

"Truly, this only I have found: That God made man upright, But they have sought out many schemes. "Eccl 7:29

Knowledge that is just full of schemes, is not 'powerful.' You can't run around calling an apple a banana, and a cat a lion, whereby you refuse to accept the difference. When you stubbornly look at life in a wicked scheme filled way, you do injustice to yourself, and to everybody around you. Your posture is not 'powerful.' Acts of these kinds, brought a lot of suffering in Uganda, Germany, China, Russia and all over the world, the perpetrators of those lies became prey to the same traps they laid for others. People lay dead on battle fields because of vain propaganda and empty glory. The values they cherished were no good for society, but only sowed discard and confusion, which leads to people fighting back instead of working in harmony. As one who has pastored a number of churches, I have come to conclude, that the aspirations of all human beings are basically the same. They are all looking for good.

Many of Idi Amin's henchmen died in the war that liberated Uganda. Others fled to the neighboring countries. Idi Amin himself, who had declared many times that he will rule Uganda for life, for he claimed 'powerful'. He kept saying he had the best brain on earth, and that he was the most professional field commander, as well as someone who feared no man, except God, ran away hastily for his life in 1979. He stole millions of dollars and assets of the hard working people of Uganda. The knowledge he claimed that he had was no good for humanity, it only caused suffering, death, and destruction. The opposite of 'powerful.'

Signs of Weak Leadership

Any regime whereby the president of that nation puts their clansmen, tribal people, and family members in all the major positions of power, ignoring diversity in the country, is headed for a fall. It is a weak regime.

For, that kind of dictatorship lacks a solid foundation to sustain it. The perpetrators may run around disguising 'powerful' but in just a matter of time, the entire roof will come crumbling down upon them. Later to find out that all the wealth that they accumulated and the money they collected from the tax payers will never be theirs. Another sad thing about it is, the supporters of the unjust regime ends up becoming victims of the wrath of the people whom they had manipulated all along. That happened to Idi Amin's regime, Muammer Gadhafi dictatorship, etc.

This book entitled, 'The Most Powerful People on Earth,' will grace many places of power, for the Lord God Almighty had this book written to help us do the right thing, and end up with abundant life. Jesus said, in the Holy Bible, in the book of John Chapter Ten that "The thief does not come except to steal, and to kill, and to destroy. I have come that they may have life, and that they may have it more abundantly." John 10:10 God loves everybody and does not desire for anyone to perish. The Bible says, the love of money is the root of all evil. It is not saying that we should not have money, but that money should not have us. It should not become the controlling power over our lives. Instead

We must be love driven, looking out for the best in everyone, for it takes the efforts of everybody for us to be able to meet our destiny. Nobody is self-made. We all thrive on the efforts and sacrifices of one another. The people God used to stop the carnage of Idi Amin, Adolf Hitler and many others of that kind, were men and women like you and me who believed in all of us. So, treating people with contempt and supposedly being stealthy is not 'powerful' but a very clear proof that one is weak and full of fear. Whatever is controlling that person is not the Spirit of God, but the spirit of fear, which is demonic.

Our pursuing of 'Powerful' through knowledge as students

After four years at St. Henry's College, that which was described as ordinary level, we had to do exams in order to join the advanced level. The advanced level is for a duration of two years in Uganda. That is when you tend to narrow down towards your specialty. For example, if you are going to study engineering, you may need a combination of: mathematics, chemistry, and physics or Applied Mathematics, Pure Mathematics and Physics. We abbreviate those combinations as PCM or PMM. Let's say that you are interested in becoming a physician. You had to take physics, biology and chemistry; this combination is referred to as PCB. There were so many other combinations, like HEL which is history, economics, and literature; GEM – that is geography, economics and mathematics. Through this kind of knowledge, one may become a judge, an attorney, engineer, politician, medical doctor, philosopher, teacher, architect, mechanic, geologist, etc.

Personally, I was and I am very gifted in the sciences. So, I took physics, applied mathematics, pure mathematics and chemistry. The combination, PMM, was only offered at St. Henry's College, at that time. Most other colleges had PCM instead, and for one to be accepted in that class, you needed to have a very 'powerful' understanding of mathematics in any form.

Many of those students who enrolled in that combination, were considered to be geniuses, and that is how we perceived ourselves. We thought we were very powerful people undergirded by knowledge!!!

We walked around with our noses up, shoulders stretched out, acting like the progress of the whole world was at our fingertips, and that we could solve any complicated problem. We had an attitude of victory. Our teachers encouraged us so much by saying to us, 'With Knowledge you can live anywhere on earth and be prosperous, as well as help others have good success, irrespective of where you come from, or where you were born.' Chemistry was added also to our class. Since I am a preacher now, as well as an author, let me update you on how I would say this, for someone who really wants to do exploits. "Those who do wickedly against the covenant he shall corrupt with flattery; but the people who know their God shall be strong, and carry out *great exploits*." Dan 10:32 Beloved, the good news is, anyone who is willing to embrace the word of God, the Holy Bible, and in that way gets to know God, automatically qualifies for exploits.

I have to admit that the students in our class in Uganda, Africa were very sharp and smart. We were very prudent, hardworking and very competitive. We spent most of our time solving very difficult mathematical and scientific problems. We had knowledge, and we loved working with it. You could not just walk to any one of us and say you are jokers, or you are not that gifted and expect that to work. No, no. We could look at you as 'crazy.' We really believed that we had the ingenuity to design anything, as well as create something to make the world a better place to live in.

We spent most of our time solving mathematical problems, as students almost all of our tasks were about how to calculate equations. We loved physics, I personally would score very high in that subject. It was like a wonder world to all of us.

We felt great about ourselves; the crème of the earth. We would apply this knowledge to our daily lives, bring it to our daily lives during holidays, to us science was not a mystery but something to delight in. I frequently applied these scientific ideas on our ranch.

The Lord is leading me to share part of my testimony with you, so that you understand that this book is not trying to undermine anything or anyone, but it is about truth. We are getting to the truth by God's grace. Bishop Leonard Kayiwa has lived real life like you and experienced the ups and downs of life. When he shares with you events in this book, he really brings it to a solid reality; that will ignite your spirit to fruitfulness.

I fully believe that right now you are asking, "Who are the most powerful people on earth?" How can I know them and how do they benefit my life. Could I be part of those people, or how can I become part of the most powerful people on earth, and what shall I have to be so; how much does it cost, where is it, what is it that I need to become that powerful so that I may help a lot of people?

The ability to conquer everything around you, ability to solve any problem, and make things happen without you being able to conquer your 'self' (that is your flesh) is not 'powerful.' The Bible says, the works of the flesh are evident, *"Now the works of the flesh are evident, which are: adultery, fornication, uncleanness, lewdness, idolatry, sorcery, hatred, contentions, jealousies, outbursts of wrath, selfish ambitions, dissensions, heresies, envy, murders, drunkenness, revelries, and the like; of which I tell you beforehand, just as I also told you in time past, that those who practice such things will not inherit the kingdom of God." Gal 5:19-21*

Beloved, on this note I leave you to examine yourself, are you full of yourself, do you have the ability to do to others what you want them to do to you? How do people feel when they are around you, do they feel loved, honored, celebrated, accepted, motivated, great?

EL-SHADDAI

GOD

ALMIGHTY

2

POWER

"And the whole multitude sought to touch Him, for power went out from Him and healed them all." Luke 10:19

What is Power, Why Power, Do we have to have Power, Where does Power dwell?

This book is about the most powerful people on earth revealed, and we have to do justice to this very important subject. I already know that some of you reading this book are part of other beliefs, rather than the Holy Bible. The Bible may not be a book you are familiar with, and that is very understandable. With that in mind, do not forget that you are on this journey with a pastor who spent most of his time at colleges, universities, schools, studying mathematics, physics and chemistry, as well as engineering, theology, divinity, various languages as well as psychology.

The word 'power,' was very common in my books of study, and I did a lot of calculations regarding '**power**' equations, and I am very conversant with many theories out there. Know that we are going to get to the crest of this. I am completely convinced that, for something to be 'powerful' it must have power in all aspects; that is in societies, nations, continents and all areas of influence. For example, that which causes bulbs to light, most ovens to heat up and cook, elevators to move up and down, street lights to shine, door bells to ring, etc., is referred to as power. When people see no action when those equipment, are turned on, they simply say, there is no power. I have lived on three continents: North America, Asia and Africa and found the description to be the same.

'Power' has brought amazing changes in human society. It reminds me of the scripture in the Book of James in the Holy Bible, chapter number one, verse seventeen, "Every good gift and every perfect gift is from above, and comes down from the Father of lights, with whom there is no variation or shadow of turning." James 1:17

Lines of electric power ran across the whole earth. It is as if the whole world is wired up. In the country of my original birth, Uganda, Africa, due to the fact that river Nile originates from Uganda, there happens to be a very big dam at the City of Jjinja. The turbans that generate electricity at that location are very big and very

Power

wide. Tourists come from all over the world to behold this famous scene of smoke-like mist due to water falling from a very high cliff, and embarking on a journey to the north of Africa. Power lines run from Jjinja to so many places in East Africa. Uganda gets paid for selling electrical power to neighboring countries. The church I pastored in Kampala, was in very close proximity to these amazing lines. We always gazed at them in amazement. The poles had signs on them, "Do not touch, danger."

'Power' in the form of electricity is one of the major forces behind the success of any major project in the world. Be it in hospitals, industries, governments, educational facilities, travel, motor vehicles and planes, it is really part of the survival of the human race. This makes this subject very relevant today, for you have to have 'power,' in order to be identified with 'the most powerful people on earth.'

On a certain day in the United States of America, power went out in a very major city, it was winter, and very cold. Due to that power outage, some people died, travel by plane was cancelled, the subways had to be closed, and many could not go to places due to the absence of power. I am taking time to look at reality with you in a very simple analysis. I have avoided being very scientific for I don't believe the subject I am dealing with here in this book should be that complex.

Man has also learned how to store power in batteries as well as have some simple way of generating it. This thing I am talking to you about is invisible. It is capable of moving from one point to another point through conductors. It can also be very dangerous when mishandled as well as applied wrongly. I am very familiar with that kind of power and its effects. I understand the composition of electrons and neutrons and, their molecular structure. So I can be a good guide in this subject 'power.'

My Experience with Another Kind of 'Power'

I was a student at Hahai University in Nanjing, China, studying Irrigation and Water Conservation Engineering. God had graced me with a full scholarship from the government of China, as an international student. I received a check every month from the People's Republic of China, as pocket money to help me take care of my needs at the university. We lived in the residences on campus. It was a time of much study and research. This was my first time to experience extreme weather changes. The country I grew up in, Uganda, Africa, is right at the equator and it has equatorial climate. The equator runs right through my place of birth, we never had hot summers or cold winters. What we have is dry and rainy seasons.

When I arrived in China, I came in contact with these biting weather conditions. Thank God for electrical 'power.' Electrical power kept us warm in winter and cool during the summer. I was accustomed to a climate where most houses did not need to use heating or cooling systems. One would just open the windows or close them, depending on what was comfortable. During my time of study in Uganda, from primary school to the university, we never had to use a central cooling nor heating system, for the weather conditions were not extreme at all. Well, let me introduce you to this other power, and how I found out about it.

A Medical Professor Lends Me a Book, Titled "The Holy Spirit"

I was a 'born again' Christian then. That means, I had received Jesus Christ as my personal savior. "But as many as received Him, to them He gave the right to

The Most Powerful People on Earth Revealed

Become the children of God; to those who believe in His name." John 1:12, I had done that when I was a first year student at Makerere University in Uganda, resident in Lumumba Hall, Kampala, on the continent of Africa.

A fellow student whose major was engineering, introduced me to the scriptures in the Holy Bible regarding 'born again.' "There was a man of the Pharisees named Nicodemus, a ruler of the Jews. This man came to Jesus by night and said to Him, "Rabbi, we know that you are a teacher come from God; for no one can do these signs that you do unless God is with him." Jesus answered and said to him, "Most assuredly. I say to you. Unless one is born again, he cannot see the Kingdom of God." John 3:1-3

He and his friend talked to me about another power, which they claimed to be an authority that gives you a higher status and authority, as well as heavenly rights when received, which is of the kingdom of God. There were two in the room, and they insisted that I needed to become, "born again." Saying, that what Paul wrote in the book of First Corinthians 4:20, could be experienced by human beings. "For the Kingdom of God is not in words, but in power." 1Cor 4:20. Well, I entered China, a 'born-again' Christian.

How I Received a Book That Introduced Me to The Dimension of Power I Had Never Dreamed Of

I had visited the University of Medicine in Nanjing. There was a student from Uganda, he was a 'born again' Christian; which means 'Omulokole' in Luganda –a saved person. As we talked, it came into his heart to introduce me to one of the professors at his school of medicine. This man was a lecturer from the U.S.A., and specialized in internal medicine.

The two of us went and visited with him. You may realize, we were right in the heart of China and it was the Chinese language that was spoken all around us; we studied in Chinese, communicated with one another in Chinese, so it was very refreshing to be meeting someone who speaks English. In East Africa, most of our studies, were done in English.

There were so many books in his residence, and among them, I saw a book with the title, 'The Holy Spirit.' It really caught my attention. This was a very kind and courteous man. He prepared for us nice tea, and very delicious Chinese food. Meanwhile, I got the courage to ask him if I could borrow his book about the

Holy Spirit, and amazing enough, he was more than happy to let me have it. He said that, the Lord Jesus Christ said, "Give to him who asks you, and from him who wants to borrow from you, do not turn away." Matt 5:42 He let me have the book, on the authority of the word of God, and that was fascinating to me.

What I Found in the Book and How It Impacted Me

Being a student of Engineering, I was accustomed to researching and proving things. You could not just walk to me and pour an idea or a thought down my throat. You had to explain what you had, to the depth, with figures and numbers as well as genuine experiments and theories to support your position.

I looked at this book in a very analytical way, wondering whether there was anything in it for me, for really if I needed any book, outside of my field of study, it had to be such that it empowers me to excel in my engineering profession

The author of this book, to me was very mathematical; very candid about the subject of the Holy Spirit, and applied testimonies, as well as scriptures from the Holy Bible to make his point. He emphasized

Especially Jesus' words in the book of Acts, "But you shall receive power when the Holy Spirit has come upon you; and you shall be witnesses to Me in Jerusalem and in all Judea and Samaria, and to the end of the earth." Acts 1:8

What is this 'Power' Jesus is Talking About?

Just looking at that scripture above, you can actually see the effects of power right there. You and I know, when power of any kind is in force, there has to be effects. It will affect something when you apply power to a vehicle, it moves. It starts, makes noise, lights come on, doors can open and close. When power is applied to a T.V. set, it comes on, lights up. It can also be applied to a patient in a hospital on life support. In the case of Acts 1:8, this power energizes the recipients to be witnesses of the death and resurrection of the Lord Jesus Christ. Something happened to these people, supernaturally, and turns them into lively witnesses.

How I Arrived at the Decision to Have this 'Power'

I read the book thoroughly, without any bias, and I came to the conclusion that everybody alive needed this

'Power'. Where I was in China, that is Nanjing, there were no evangelical churches. You could not just step off the campus and find Bible believing congregations. Nearly 98% of my fellow students, especially the Chinese, had been told that God was not there. Many of them, their goal was to study hard, get a degree, find a wife or a husband, have a place to call home, with a good job, and live until you are gathered to the earth, fulfilling God's word to mankind in the book of Genesis: "In the sweat of your face ye shall eat bread Till you return to the ground, For out of it you were taken; For dust you are, And to dust you shall return." Gen 3:19

The 'Born Again' Medical Science Professor Recommends to me to Visit the New Covenant Church in Hong Kong

I went back to the gentleman from whom I had borrowed the book, titled 'The Holy Spirit.' I let him know that I had read everything in that book, with a Bible on my side, and I did agree with the author entirely. Therefore, I need to have the Baptism of the Holy Spirit with evidence of speaking in other tongues.

I want to let you know, that if this kind of 'power' is really there, I was determined to find out. I had to have this power. Especially after fully being convinced and persuaded by the author of that wonderful book, that this experience of the Baptism of the Holy Spirit with evidence of speaking in tongues was for any willing person, who desired to make a difference on the earth and the world. That lined up very well with my ambitions, and that is why I was at the university learning.

The Promise is to All

Then Peter said to them, "Repent, and let every one of you be baptized in the name of Jesus Christ for the remission of sins; and you shall receive the gift of the Holy Spirit. For the promise is to you and to your children, and to all who are afar off, as many as the Lord our God will call." Acts 2:38-39

As a Bishop, and someone God has graced to teach the Word of God, as well as to pray for numerous people, I have come to conclude that many times, people are where they are in their beliefs, because of what they know, or what they don't know. No wonder Jesus Christ said, "And you shall know the truth, and the truth shall set you free." John 8:32 You, the person reading this book, by now you might have so many questions in regard to the subject of the Holy Spirit. Well, I have good news for you. One of these days, I will write a book entitled, 'The Holy Spirit,' but as for now, let's deal with this subject, 'power' in our quest for 'The most powerful people on the earth revealed'.

The brother in Christ, who gave me the book, by virtue that he was a 'born-again believer' like me, in line with this scripture "who were born, not of blood, nor of the will of a man, but of God." John 1:13 We were getting along very well. He was from the United States of America, and I was from Uganda, Africa. Our shades were different, but we completely knew we were of the same family. The Family of God, and our uniqueness was for God's glory.

I am reminded, growing up on our homestead, we had all kinds of animals, goats, sheep, cows, rabbits, dogs, cats, deer, pigs, and a variety of fowls including chickens, ducks, turkeys, as well as fish in the water, for we owned a five square mile ranch. We also owned a farm near our house. That gave me the opportunity to see the family of all these different creatures, for example; a chicken could lay eggs and produce twenty little chicks, some yellow, black, white, red, maroon, of course every chicken has some other colors as part of the way they were divinely created. Basically, fitting in the description of the word 'colored.' I just like that rainbow mixture, it is astounding to behold. It makes your day. I saw that with puppies and piglets. What about fish...well, God is amazing! I also want to bring this to your attention. Human being are colored, they have more than one color on their bodies. Look at your palms, hair, eyes, fingernails, toe nails, teeth, tongue and lips. Isn't it amazing that God loves coloring things. We have a bird in Uganda, called cranes, that bird is amazingly colored, it even has a crest on its head, which is colored as well. You can find it on the Uganda flag.

This very generous professor of medicine, at Nanjing University of Medicine referred me to a friend of his in Hong Kong, China. One whom he said was full of the power of the Holy Spirit; having joy and peace. He attended a Pentecostal church, out there on the island of Kowloon in Hong Kong. So, I was to travel to meet him during the summer break.

On the Way to the Island of Kowloon, Hong Kong, China

I took a train from Nanjing to the ocean harbor, then

The Most Powerful People on Earth Revealed

I boarded a ferry on its way to Hong Kong from the mainland of China. I was seeking, "Ask, and it will be given to you, seek and you will find, knock and it will be opened to you." Matthew 7:7 I was accustomed to seeking, that is how I ended up at East China University of Irrigation and Water Conservation Engineering, these days referred to as Hahai University; seeking knowledge. This venture fitted very well in my mathematical life style. You had to work on the equation until you arrived at the solution, so I had to come into an encounter with this other 'power.'

Upon arrival, I was received at Hong Kong by the vice president of the Baptist University in Hong Kong, he welcomed me to his home. They were wonderful people. He and his wife furnished me with a very nice room in the skyscraper where they lived. This precious couple were originally from Britain, and were also 'Born again' Christians. I felt their love. 'He who loves his brother abides in the light, and there is no stumbling in him.' I John 2:10 They were willing to take me to any place I needed to get to. The professor at the Medical University Nanjing Clinic was my divine connection to these people of God.

My First Meeting was among people full of Joy, Peace and Power

There was a gathering at a Christian family's home on Kowloon Island. We went there by boat. It was a very interesting experience. In my quest to have an encounter with the 'power,' the one I had read about in the Bible, through the book titled, 'The Holy Spirit.'

These people were from all walks of life, and loved one another. They seemed to be full of love and joy, treated one another with honor. Some were from the United States of America, Korea, Japan, England, China, Russia, Singapore, Nepal, Mexico, etc. I was amazed to see the brotherly love of Jesus manifested. "By this all will know that you are my disciples if you have love for one another." John 13:35

This alone, convinced me that there was something supernatural empowering those Saints to have such affection for one another. They operated as a family, they celebrated one another and held everyone in high esteem. I felt welcome and loved.

Beloved, this book is for everyone who can dare believe that there is more. It is for dreamers like you, seekers of the truth, and those who can dare stand to be blessed. It is a book handed out to all people without any bias, and the testimonies as well as incidences presented in here are part of what makes this book a must read. This is a gem in your possession, right now. It is something you must tell everybody about. It contains a message for all humanity; a message of hope.

These believers that I met at their fellowship, told me that they were filled with the Holy Spirit. They let me know that, one needs 'power' in order to be an effective witness. "But you shall receive power when the Holy Spirit has come upon you; and you shall be witnesses to Me in Jerusalem, and in all Judea and Samaria, and to the ends of the earth." Acts 1:8

My Next Stop: The New Covenant Church in Hong Kong

The next place I went to was the New Covenant Church in Hong Kong, China. It was a Sunday morning, around 10:0am. The service was in a very nice sanctuary, the worship and praise was amazing. Most of the attendants that day were Chinese and many could speak English. There were other people there from other countries. I found a place to sit, right at the front pew. I was making sure that I am in the center of it all-I had to get what I came for. The preacher that day was a visiting evangelist/pastor from the United States of America. He was very fiery, and bold. His preaching was with a lot of authority. He seemed to believe 100% in what he was communicating to the people. I could feel power – something divine and powerful in that place. I was convinced that it must be that other 'power.' Not electric power, nor human power, but that which I had read about in the book.

I Approached the Preacher

So after the service was over, I asked the pastor of that church if they could pray with me to be filled with the Holy Spirit with evidence of speaking in tongues, like what happened in the book of Acts, "While Peter was still speaking these words, the Holy Spirit fell upon all those who heard the word. And those of the circumcision who believed were astonished, as many as came with Peter, because the gift of the Holy Spirit had been poured out on the Gentiles also. For they heard them speak with other tongues and magnify God. Then Peter answered, "Can anyone forbid water, that these should not be baptized who have received the Holy Spirit, just as we have?" Acts 10:44-47

Power Has Effects

Peter and those believers that he came with seems to

understand the effects of 'power', for power causes things to happen, for example: when heat goes through an element, it can cause expansion, melting, evaporation, or the opposite can occur. In case it leaves that object, it can be metal, water, air, etc. In this event, people are speaking in tongues – heavenly language, by supernatural power. This is similar to what I saw in the New Covenant Church that day. People everywhere were speaking in a heavenly language. I also saw them praying for the sick, to receive healing and the people did receive their healing. There was so much power in that place until people who were being prayed for could literally be vibrating as if they were in contact with a live electrical circuit. I witnessed all of that.

I Receive That 'Power'

The pastor of the church asked the visiting preacher with him, and other believers, to pray for me to receive the Baptism of the Holy Spirit with evidence of speaking in tongues. They were all in agreement. "Again I say to you that if two of you agree on earth concerning anything that they ask, it will be done for them by my Father in heaven." Matt 18:19 They led me to a chapel within the church. We all knelt down with

Power

Hands lifted up. The visiting preacher was holding one of my hands up as we prayed.

"He said, Father, Lord God, we do ask that
You will fill this brother of ours, Leonard
Kayiwa with the blessed Holy Spirit and
Endow him with power from above.
Precious Jesus Christ, baptize him with
The Holy Spirit, with evidence of speaking
In tongues."

Immediately 'power' goes throughout my whole entire body!!!

While he was still praying, I suddenly felt like a rock was all around me. My hands could not come down. It was like I was engrafted in a rock. No wonder the Bible calls Jesus the Rock of our Salvation. All my theories in science were challenged by this experience. I just felt a presence of this invisible rock all around me. It was as if I was hewn in this rock.

After the first experience, I felt like I was connected to a live electric current from the top of my head to the bottom of my feet. It was so powerful, I was literally vibrating under this other 'power.' It seemed as if I was becoming a new man. There was something cleansing about this experience. I became energized supernaturally. This surpassed all the physics, mathematics, chemistry I had learned in the engineering class, at the university, and the years before. This extraordinary power did not hurt me, but it was life giving. I had never experienced anything of that magnitude before.

Laughter Follows

What followed after the first two encounters, was perplexing, I laughed as a baby, full of joy. Joy, joy. I mean my heart was merry, supernatural joy was all over me, "A merry heart does good, like medicine, But a broken spirit dries the bones." Prov 17:20. There was something very healing about that laughter. It was like somebody was causing a nice warmth to go throughout my body. It was a healing experience. Then suddenly, my lips supernaturally started talking to me prophetically. What amazed me, these words that were being formed on my lips, were not of my making, my mouth was saying things about me which I knew were true, and no one else in that room could know that, except me. The words were about my history and all the trials I have faced, which God delivered me from. This operation was surely divine, only God could do that. This lead me to believe that God is real and has absolute power, and man is no match to God. No wonder the scripture says, "The king's heart is in the hand of the Lord, Like the rivers of water; He turns it wherever He wishes." Prov 21:1

God caused my mouth to talk to me. My mouth was completely in His hands, words about my future, my past, were just coming forth. One of the things that I heard clearly was when God said, "You shall put the deepest truth into words by revelation knowledge, and many shall be drawn to the love of God through your life." It is very possible that my writing of books is part of the fulfillment of that word.

My brother, my sister, beloved of God who is reading this book, God is real, and this other 'power' I am sharing with you, is very, very real. That touch made a believer out of me.

Suddenly I Started Speaking in Tongues with Interpretation

I began speaking in tongues with interpretation; this is how it happened. I could speak words in unknown tongues, right from my heart given to my lips, and this would be followed by English words. It was as if utterances were made for me, and then delivered to my mouth to speak. Meanwhile, a divine presence was all around me. Part of what was taking place, had a similitude to the Word of God that came to Jeremiah in Chapter Eighteen, from verse one to verse two, "The word which came to Jeremiah from the Lord, saying, "Arise and go down to the potter's house, and there I will cause you to hear My words." Jer 18:1-2 My coming to the New Covenant Church service that Sunday morning, must have been the leading of the Holy Spirit.

I believe the Gifts of the Holy Spirit were manifesting through me right then, "But the manifestation of the Spirit is given to each one for the profit of all. For one is given the word of wisdom, through the Spirit, to another the word of knowledge through the same Spirit, to another faith by the same Spirit, to another gifts of healing by the same Spirit, to another the working of miracles, to another prophecy, too another discernment of spirits, to another different kinds of tongues, to another the interpretation of tongues." 1 Cor 12:7-10

Being someone who was born in Uganda, and speaking Luganda as my initial language, and where else I had to learn other languages, I perceived the magnitude of this miracle of being able to speak in unknown tongues, without having learned it in school, and being so fluent with it in just a moment, was without a doubt, a divine act. I had to study Chinese at the International University of Languages in Beijing, China. That is how I gained control over that language. I graduated and went ahead and joined Hahai University to pursue engineering. Chinese is a tough language, especially when it comes to writing. You have to know a lot of characters for you to get much done. I am also a student of English, I studied this language and passed the exams. I do speak it, as well as write it. So, being able to speak fluently another language in tongues, which no human being has taught you, is itself a powerful mystery- that is 'power.'

When I was in China, at the university in Nanjing, I sat with the Chinese students in the same lecture rooms, and was held to the same standard as them, who grew up speaking Chinese. God helped me, and my scores at the university were very, very, high, which used to cause a number of professors to wonder. I can also hear as well as read Swahili, Lunyankole, Luchiga, Lutolo, Lunyoolo, Lusoga and some other languages. Some of these languages I learned them by association with people who spoke those dialects. However my speaking in tongues that day, was a game changer. I fluently spoke this language, as the Holy Spirit gave me utterance, for almost one hour.

Warmth Sensation

Something else happened which was remarkable, I felt a warm sensation all over my body. It was like a very nice liquid being poured all over me. Like an oil. This went on for some time. It would settle around my heart area, and again spread out throughout the whole body. 'Power' was circulating all over and all around me. The Glory of God was present. There is a scripture in the Bible, in the book of Second Chronicles, Chapter Five, whereby something of this similitude happened, "indeed it came to pass, when the trumpeters and singers were as one, to make one sound to be heard in praising and thanking the Lord, and when they lifted up their voice with the trumpets and cymbals and instruments of music, and praised the Lord, saying:

"For He is good,

For His mercy endures

Forever,

That the house, the house of the LORD, was filled with a cloud, so that the priests could not continue ministering because of the cloud; for the glory of the LORD filled the house of God."2 Chr 5:13-14

This is how I encountered the other 'power' and beloved, all you who are reading this book, I Bishop Leonard Kayiwa am telling you whole truth, and truth alone. What happened to me that day changed my life forever. I have been able to witness that power in operation all over the world, as I minister the Word of God.

There is a scripture I want to bring to your attention, in the Gospel of John, Chapter Seven, Verse Thirty-eight, "He who believes in me as the scripture has said, out of his heart will flow rivers of living water." John 7:38

I Return to Mainland China

I went back to China mainland, full of power and very highly motivated. At that time, I was enrolled in two degree programs, one was a Correspondence Bible Theology Degree Program from Brussels, Belgium in the Netherlands, and the other one was the Irrigation and Water Conservation Engineering degree program that I was in at Hahai University. I learned a lot about God and His Word through those books that were sent from Brussles, right to the mainland of China.

The Most Powerful People on Earth Revealed

This book is about the most powerful people on earth revealed. People we need to know. I remember some of the words that were said during the eulogy of the late Arch Bishop of Uganda, Mpalanyi Nkoyoyo, in Uganda at the Shrine of the Uganda Martyrs at Namugongo, Africa, where thousands gathered for a funeral service that lead to his final burial place.

Exempt of some of the very important words that were said during the eulogy of Arch Bishop Mpalanyi Nkoyoyo, a 'mulokole'(a saved person)

One of the eulogists during this state funeral, which was viewed worldwide, said, *'The reason why some of us are weeping is because we understand the blessedness of having this kind of person in our neighborhood, country, continent, and community. So, his passing is a great loss to all of us. This Bishop loved people and God, and he wished well for all of us. This man honored the men who were martyred for the cause of the Gospel, and their love for Jesus. No wonder he is being buried right here in the place where millions come to, from all over the world to celebrate those believers who through their martyrdom, the world became a better place, and these people today are rightly referred to as saints."* This born again man, was given a state funeral, which implies that somehow every Ugandan contributed something to his honor and his appreciation. Much was said by different individuals regarding his kind acts to humanity. Precious people of God, we need those kinds of people in the world of today.

We all want people with 'power' around us. They can shape positively the direction of events. They can also bring civilization to our communities. In a world where extremism is part of the norm; some people calling a banana an apple, calling yellow, white, chocolate color black, blue as green: whereby they have abandoned honesty, and they are raging with fury and hate, completely out of control. A world where supremists are raging with a rotten world view and are literally injecting confusion in communities.

Religious extremism and dangerous political ideologies which are very polarizing, are being practiced by people who confuse wickedness for 'power', which actually is no power at all, but attributes of wickedness. The Bible puts it this way, "For the earnest expectation of the creation eagerly waits for the revealing of the sons of God. For the creation was subjected to futility, not willingly, but because of Him who subjected it in hope because the creation itself also will be delivered from the bondage of corruption into the glorious liberty of the children of God." Rom 8:19-21 It is very difficult for somebody to love somebody else, if they can't even love themselves. What a person says, reveals their heart, for a tree is judged by its fruits. Make the tree good, and the fruit will be good.

God does not see us as man sees; He looks at the heart. God said this to Prophet Samuel in the Holy Bible, when the Lord sent him to the house of Jesse to anoint a king for Israel, instead of Saul, "But the Lord said to Samuel, "Do not look at his appearance or at his physical stature, because I have rejected him. For the Lord does not see as man sees, for man looks at the outward appearance, but the Lord looks at the heart." I Sam 16:7. Context matters, and good judgment is important, for by it you can have a right application to the situation under examination; what we are examining now is 'power.' Please stay with me. We are going to get to the bottom of this!

Power Went Out of Him – That is Jesus

My opening scripture describes a scenario where Jesus Christ was in a certain place "And He came down with them and stood on a level place with a crowd of

His disciples and a great multitude of people from all Judea and Jerusalem, and from the sea coast of Tyre and Sidon, who came to hear Him and be healed of their diseases." Luke 6:17 The reason why all these people came to where Jesus Christ the Son of the living God was, it was because of what they had found in Him; one who loves helping, comforting, exalting, edifying, and speaking to people, good words of life.

The moment they heard of the things He was doing in their community; they became attracted to the person of Jesus Christ. Some of you reading this book may say, well, we are with you on a lot of subjects, you have unfolded in this book. But we don't believe Jesus is a son of God. Well, I have found this discrepancy especially among the people of the Moslem faith, and the argument presented is that God cannot have a son, though in the same breath they say, God can do all things or anything is possible with God.

This is my conclusion. God can have a Son, and does have a Son. His name is Jesus Christ. In case you are of a different faith reading this book, and you were told that God cannot have a Son, please put away those false teachings, and only continue with me on this adventurous ride. There is more revelation coming.

The Most Powerful People on Earth Revealed

These people walked miles to get where Jesus was. Some rode on donkeys; others were actually carried to that place by friends, they were sick and could not walk. Others had to get on boats and then walk to where this 'powerful' man was. They held off their other pressing obligations in order to go and hear His sayings. For His sayings appealed to the real core of their being, and made them better people.

This is the person you would want and like to be in your life, for your real needs to be met. "For the law was given through Moses, but grace and truth came through Jesus Christ." John 1:17

The Bible continues to indicate that some of those who came to Jesus had complications that no medical science could ever resolve, nor electrical power or fire power, could remove. Some of these people were under torment of invisible forces – devils and demons; something you can't get your hands on in the natural. Human armies can't defeat it, philosophical ideas cannot subdue them, something you can't subdue with empty words. You have to have the other 'power.'

Let Us Look at this Example

Now God worked unusual miracles by the hands of Paul, so that even handkerchiefs or aprons were brought from his body to the sick, and the diseases left them and the evil spirits went out of them. Then some of the Itinerant Jewish exorcists, took it on themselves to call the name of the Lord Jesus over those who had evil spirits, saying, "We exorcise you by the Jesus whom Paul preaches." Also there were Seven Sons of Sceva, a Jewish Chief Priest, who did so. And the evil spirit answered and said, "Jesus I know, and Paul I know, but who are you?" Acts 19:11-15

It is obvious what this evil spirit was questioning: was there authority; it is about authorization and 'power'. For what follows is very profound, "Then the man in whom the evil spirit was leaped on them, over powered them, and prevailed against them, so that they fled out of that house naked and wounded. This became known both to all Jews and Greeks dwelling in Ephesus; and fear fell on them all, and the name of the Lord Jesus was magnified." Acts 19:16-17 You have to have that kind of power that was with Paul in order to displace demons and devils, as well as undo the works of the enemy. God sent me to show you something magnificent. We will arrive to a good conclusion regarding 'power'. Those Sons of Sceva were not part of those people who operate at a higher level. If being a Jew was the qualification for them to bring deliverance to one suffering under torment of evil spirits, then the man would have been freed through their words. But, it is very, very clear in these scriptures that being Jews never qualified them to cast out those devils. They had to be 'born again' Christian believers who are described in Luganda, a language spoken in Uganda, Africa as 'balokole'(meaning saved ones or born again believers).

Let us continue with Jesus' narrative.

The Bible says that people were brought to Jesus that day with all kinds of infirmities, "as well as those who were tormented with unclean spirits. And they were healed." Luke 6:18

'Power' went out of Jesus Christ!!!

"And the whole multitude sought to touch Him, for power went out from Him and healed them all." Luke 6:19 Precious reader of this book, for someone to do justice to the topic of this book, one has to understand 'power,' I want to try to define it as the ability to get something done or bring an authoritative change to circumstances, or that which can drastically change the course of an event. In this Bible story, this power had very positive results. It brought wholeness to those who came in contact with it, many were freed instantly from demonic operations; sorcery and witchcraft. We need this virtue today and thanks to God it is available to whoever is willing to be blessed and turned into a blessing.

Power Descends on the People During Our Worship Service in Kamwokya, Africa

It was a Wednesday Miracle Worship Service at Christian Faith Center, Kamwokya, near Mawamda Road in the nation of Uganda, which is part of the East African community. Where the Swahili language stands out as the majority spoken in that region. I had been counseling the people of God the entire day. My schedule was like this: Very early in the morning, people were seated in line to come and pray with me. Whenever I counseled with the people of God, I would point them to the Word of God in the Bible.

The people of God needed something powerful to keep, as well as have in order to sustain their miracle from God. A word they could stand on in their day to day affairs – and that is the Word of God. The scriptures declare, "For the word of God is living and

Powerful, and sharper than any two-edged sword, piercing even to the division of soul and spirit, and is a discerner of the thought's and intents of the heart." Heb 4:12

The Anointing; that is the supernatural power of God was present

Power was going out to these people who needed a touch from God; yokes were being broken and burdens removed. This was a fulfillment of the Word of God. "It shall come to pass in that day, That his burden will be taken away from your shoulder, And his yoke from your neck, And the yoke will be destroyed because of the anointing oil." Is 10:27

This power, referred to as the anointing, relieves people from hurts and pains. At about 5:30pm, that day, it was time for the evening worship service. People started taking their seats in the Sanctuary. Ministers took their position at the podium. Our church had the five-fold ministry operating. We had anointed evangelists, teachers, pastors, apostles, and prophets, within our congregation. "And He Himself gave some to be apostles, some prophets, some evangelists, and some pastors and teachers, for the equipping of the saints for the work of ministry, for the edifying of the body of Christ, till we all come to the unity of the faith and of the knowledge of the Son of God, to a perfect man, to the measure of the stature of the fullness of Christ;." Eph 4:11-13. Those in the choir sat at the raised platform behind the podium. The service began with very powerful prayer, then followed strong heavenly praise, topped with glorious worship.

The Glory of the Lord Manifests

I was still on my feet, with my hands raised to the heavens, worshipping God Almighty, when I felt a presence all around the sanctuary. It was as if the whole place was charged by an electrical like power. Suddenly, people started screaming out with joy and when I opened my eyes to see, I saw the effects of that glorious atmosphere. People were literally vibrating under the invisible power of God, others were lying on the floor of the church, laughing in the Holy Spirit.

Some were jumping up and down thanking God. This unusual experience went on for almost one hour. I just looked, I could not say anything then. The Glory of the Lord was beautifully present. This reminds me of what happened in the book of Second Chronicles, "indeed it came to pass, when the trumpeters and singers were as one, to make one sound to be heard in

Praising and thanking the Lord, and when they lifted up their voice with the trumpets and cymbals and instruments of music, and praised the Lord, saying: "For He is good, For His mercy endures forever," that the house, the house of the LORD, was filled with a cloud, so that the priests could not continue ministering because of the cloud; for the glory of the Lord filled the house of God." 2 Chr 5:11-14 I could not minister, I was numbed , that power was all over me.

There were a number of people who could not even move their legs or arms, they were as if frozen. Personally, I was slightly afraid of this power; healings broke out that day, deliverance followed, some creative miracles happened, all kinds of testimonies followed. The service went on until 1:00 a.m. in the morning. Many people just sat there, basking in the Glory of the Lord, all the way till morning. Beloved, that is power.

A Man Delivered from Food Cravings that Night

There was a man who had attended that service, who had come from Entebbe, a city where the international airport is located, as well as the state house. He was a married man, and weighed about 300 pounds. He was really overweight. I saw the power of God descend on him during the Miracle Worship Service. You could notice that he was vibrating under the power of the Holy Spirit, all the way down from his lifted hands, to his feet. He swayed under the power like a leaf of a reed. The anointing was all over him. I knew a miracle was taking place.

That day he testified that something divine went through him with a cleansing effect. He felt cleansed. It was a warmth-like presence with a soothing effect. Something which revitalized all his cells. It had a quickening like effect. "But if the Spirit of Him who raised Jesus from the dead dwells in you, He who raised Christ from the dead will also give life to your mortal bodies through His Spirit who dwells in you." Rom. 8:11.

This man came back to our church after three weeks. He looked different, he had lost most of the weight that was on him. He told the congregation that he believes the yoke of bad cravings for food, that day was broken. His wife, who came with him, testified to the same fact, that his eating habits were all altered; she got a healthy husband back.

This believer said that a number of junk foods his body was craving for before that glorious experience no longer appealed to him anymore. That he even no longer wants those foods to be put on his table. They no longer smell good to him at all, that something supernatural had happened to his metabolism. This man in about 6 months, his weight came down to nearly 150 pounds.

At the Right Hand of 'Power'

In Mark, fourteen, verse sixty-two, we find a very interesting reference to 'power' by one of the most peculiar persons who ever lived on earth – Jesus Christ. He was talking to a group of leaders who believed that they had some type of ability to make things happen. Those were the priests, religious rulers, counselors and statesmen. They were frustrated in the fact that Jesus Christ was teaching and leading people without having been authorized by them. He never attended their schools and was not at all under their jurisdiction. However, all people were going after Him, because of His life filled sayings, and healing power.

They were questioning the source of His authority, like people do today. I remember when I began pastoring in 1993, some religious people became very upset with me, for believers were leaving their churches to come to our simple place of worship, to hear the word of God and be healed as well. These people came from all types of denominations, the Catholics, Protestants, Presbyterians, Mormons, Jehovah Witnesses, Anglicans, Muslims, Baha'i faith, Seventh Day Adventists, etc. The priests, bishops, as well as the Imams of those religions would come to me very upset, saying, 'You have taken our people!'

These religious leaders lacked understanding of the freedom of worship, and for some hidden, wicked reasons, they took it upon themselves to believe that when you are a pastor over people, you then own them as your belongings. They claimed an unrealistic control over the people of God. Whatever they had, was not the 'power' we are talking about in this book. The 'power' that we are talking about in this book, does not take away peoples' freedom of worship.

Jesus said, "I AM. AND YOU WILL SEE THE SON OF MAN SITTING AT THE RIGHT HAND OF THE POWER, AND COMING WITH THE CLOUDS OF HEAVEN." MARK 14:62

One time, I was listening to a man on T.V. defining the three branches of government in the United States, which he referred to as powers; the Executive Branch, the Judiciary Branch, and the Legislature. He said, that they are supposed to operate independent of one another, so that misuse of power might be minimized, and that they also provide checks and balances. This is so because human beings are not angels.

Have you ever realized that any time the word 'power' is applied in terms of governance, it has to do with being able to get human beings to do something or being able to subject people to a certain norm of rules, do you notice that if you take people out of the equation, there would be no power at all? It is people who operate the guns, it is people who fly the planes, it is people who provide day to day services in every area of life. If there is no life in those people, then they can't be able to get anything done. That lets me know, that what is referred to as 'power' by nations is not the real power!

Today, we have groups of people exerting control over others, technically exploiting the efforts of peoples' labor. These people change constitutions of the nations against peoples' will, have their hands in the resources of nations, whereby they accumulate wealth at the expense of the health of their citizens. You can get an impression, that there is not enough for everybody. But, I want to let you know, that everything that God created, He created it in abundance. Whatever they claim to be power, is nothing but wickedness. These are gangs of exploiters who flourish on the tax payer's money. I have lived under dictatorships and have noticed that all that they do is manage people through terror, mistakenly giving an impression that they can survive without the good will of the people.

The Power – God

True power is kind, loving, compassionate, caring, creative, not destructible, sees all things, understands everything, is in all places at the same time, no regard for inequity, has solutions to spiritual needs, and is referred to as 'Our Father who art in Heaven' and that power is in the person of God. *"..Our Father in heaven, Hallowed be Your name. Your kingdom come. Your will be done On earth as it is in heaven. Give us this day our daily bead. And forgive us our debts, As we forgive our debtors. And do not lead us into temptation, But deliver us from the evil one. For Yours is the kingdom and the power and the glory forever. Amen." Matt 6:9-13*

3

JESUS CHRIST 'YESU' IN LUGANDA

"Then they were all amazed, so that they questioned among themselves, saying, "What is this? What new doctrine is this? For with authority, He commands even the unclean spirits, and they obey Him." Mark 1:27

Christ the King

In the nation of Uganda, East Africa – a nation that some still refer to as 'The Pearl of Africa,' due to how it quickly embraced civilization through the early missionaries who came to that region. A nation whereby, education was taken very seriously, ending up being the home of one of the most prestigious universities in the world – Makerere University, as well as other institutions of higher learning, that have produced various leaders in Africa.

Very gifted men and women from these institutions, are currently making a difference in nations around the world. There is a statue in the center of the capitol city of that country, dedicated to the honor to what you and I are soon going to agree to, that, there had never been any among the sons of man like Him – Jesus Christ.

The inscription on that huge statue is: 'Christ the King.' There is a Roman Catholic Church built right next to it, what is amazing about this monument is that all people of different religions, when they are guiding anybody to the vicinity of that location, which is near the seat of the Legislative Branch of Government – the Uganda Parliament. They would say, 'Go by Christ the King' or when you see a huge stature where it is written, 'Christ the King,' that will be the landmark to help you locate your destination.

What is amazing, at any time, something is going on in that location, people normally say, 'We are going to Christ the King to attend church services or a special ceremony,' by various groups. Even in my growing up as a child, I was amazed by the fact that people could literally just say, 'I am going to or by Christ the King.' Whether they were Moslems, Catholics, Pentecostals, Anglicans, Seventh-Day Adventists, Mormons, Jehovah Witnesses and even those who were yet to believe in God. Uganda is very proud of that monument in honor of Jesus Christ.

God does direct me to write books, and I do my best

to follow His leading, for I am a believer. This book is prepared for all people regardless of their nationality or place of origin. You may be reading this book in astonishment of what is presented before you right now, but I want you to know that you are God's person and you were created in the image of God. We have to have 'knowledge', for the scripture says, in Hosea Chapter Four, verse Six, "My people are destroyed for lack of knowledge." Hos 4:6 Three things stand out very strong in this verse: -

1) Knowledge is Needed

2) We Are God's People

3) We Are All Created in the Image of God

In this book, my task is to present to you a very constructive analysis as well as description of events and people, so that at the end of the day, you make a redemptive conclusion for yourself concerning 'The Greatest People on Earth Revealed.'

There is another landmark in Uganda, Africa, a shrine dedicated to the 45 martyrs, now referred to as Saints from Africa, by the Roman Catholic Church, the Anglican Church, the Episcopal Church and all other religious groups around the world. Millions of people

The Most Powerful People on Earth Revealed

Pilgrim to this unique site every year from Europe, North and South America, Asia, Australia, to be part of the worship services in commemoration of brave men and woman who refused to surrender to the dictatorship of wickedness of the king of the kingdom that was present in that region. These people chose to embrace Jesus Christ as their king. To them, 'Christ is the King' or let me say it this way, 'Christ was the King.'

That 'so called' king and his subordinates whose names I see not fit to mention in this worldwide book, of course, they are already buried. Dust to dust, earth to earth, the saying of God over them is "In the sweat of your face you shall eat bread Till you return to the ground, For out of it you were taken; For dust you are, And to dust you shall return." Gen 3:19

Those kind of kings who prey on people have fallen and fallen deep in the abyss. The reason why I use the word, 'so called king,' is because a true king or any reasonable person, don't kill people by burning them at the stake, thrusting spears through them, and falsely accuse them of sabotage because they are trying to worship the Lord God Almighty; which these precious people of God were doing, and ended up being killed in cold blood. The Bible says, 'do to others what you would have them do to you.' I don't believe these egotistic would offer themselves to be burned alive or be crucified for the people they lead, which only Christ the King did. That is why I personally believe that is the true king.

The king I am referring to today, seems to have changed lives, in a way which none other did. Stay with me, we have quite a lot of good grounds to cover and you are really going to enjoy this book.

People Have Unequivocally, Embraced Jesus Christ in Uganda

I am a citizen of the United States of America. I became an American National in 2014. I love the United States of America. My children have studied in the universities of America with all this being true, God also gave me the beautiful heritage of Africa.

He had me to be born in Uganda, Africa, to His glory. By the way, I would like to put a reminder for all of you readers, none of you chose where you were to be born, you just found yourself among those people and in that place of your birth. It is only God Almighty who knows why He sent you to the earth through the nation of your birth. The scope of exposure I have had enables me to look at a very wide spectrum in my writings. I speak Luganda, English, Chinese, etc., so I tend to follow closely events in Africa and China. As I write this book, right now, in 2018; 'Jesus Christ' is the most popular name mentioned and known by nearly everybody in Uganda. When you mention Him, 95% of the people would say that He is the most kind, loving, having something worth hearing, of all the people who ever lived on earth. No wonder there is a big revival going on in that nation.

The words of Jesus Christ are being handed over to the people by preachers, from pulpits, podiums, radio stations, television stations, newspapers, magazines, street ministries, and social media and are taught at numerous universities. The tolerance level for people for one another has gone up, which has led to a peaceable atmosphere in that nation. I know that nation very well, and I lived through the atrocities of dictatorships and unrest in the 1990's, whereby the then rulers had no tolerance at all for other views, and there was no respect for life.

The people over there, their world view has changed drastically, and has gone towards a positive, healthy direction, this falls in line with the story in the Bible where the religious leaders sent soldiers to arrest Jesus, but they came back to them without Him and said, "So there was a division among the people because of Him. Now some of them wanted to take Him, but no one laid hands on Him. Then the officers came to the chief priests and Pharisees, who said to them, "Why have you not brought Him?" The officers answered, "No man ever spoke like this Man!" John 7:43-46 These officers were trying to make a point, which is, 'We need this man, what he is saying is so much needed that we don't feel it is right to arrest Him.'

Jesus Christ, Loved by many in America

America is great, and its true greatness is not just in the ingenuity of its people. This is obvious to all nations on earth. The greatness of America is not just in its great buildings all over the nation, nor the assets like airplanes, ships, rockets, submarines, buses, space shuttles, very nice trains; No! No!

I have lived in the United States of America, and I would like to let you know, that these people are human beings like any other people in the world. Having come from a background of a lot of education, learning and studying in various educational institutions, in Africa, China and the United States of America, and being very gifted in engineering, as well as the subjects that under guards that discipline; mathematics, physics, chemistry,

The Most Powerful People on Earth Revealed

I tend to have a good evaluation of the cause of this greatness. I lived in China for a good number of years, studying at their universities. I also studied in the colleges and universities in Africa. I have been in Europe briefly, God has enabled me to be in those places and see as well as feel the people out there. I have some idea about what is common and different about these different territories and its people.

In the United States of America, Jesus Christ's words and teachings are taken very seriously, by a large number of people. When I first visited the United States of America in the 1990's, I was amazed by the amount of properties set aside as places of worship, in the Christian faith. They talked about Jesus Christ openly. Some of the people I met were complete strangers, but they received me as if I was a brother to their families. Even when some had a different color of skin, all they needed to know was that I loved the person of Jesus Christ - that is Jesus Christ, the King.

These people lived by Jesus' words, expressed through their generosity, and abided by His commandments. "And you shall love the LORD your God with all your heart..., And the second like it is this, 'You shall love your neighbor as yourself.' There is no other commandment greater than this one." Mark 12:31

Jesus Christ, 'Yesu' in Luganda

Amazing Hospitality

These people – the Americans, received me in their homes. I sat at tables with them as if I was a member of the family. They treated me with respect and they had respect for one another. Their world view was very healthy. They had joy and peace in their lives. Are you surprised that America is what it is today because of these kind of people? I believe that what has made this nation so prosperous is their embracing of the teachings of Jesus Christ. Of course there are some among them who are yet to celebrate as well as receive the person of Jesus Christ.

Imagine what the world would be like if the amount of gun fire power in the United States was controlled by people who had no regard of the teachings of Jesus Christ, like this one, "Therefore, whatever you want men to do to you, do also to them. For this is the law and the prophets." Matt 7:12

The Son of Man, Jesus Christ

Some say that Jesus Christ was a mere man, but with great values. Many in places like India, China, Persia, Korea, and Russia where there form of government differs from other countries in the West, they still reach out for a number of teachings by Jesus Christ for the well-being of their communities. In countries like Saudi Arabia, Turkey, The Arab Emirates, Libya, Egypt, and many that have a large presence of the Islamic Faith, they say that Jesus Christ is a great prophet. They believe also that He is alive with God. Whatever way you look at it, Jesus Christ is the most powerful Son of Man that ever lived.

Consider this, in the book of Matthew, Chapter nine, verse six, and see what you can make out of it in regard to this paralytic man. "But Jesus knowing their thoughts, said, "Why do you think evil in your hearts? "For which is easier, to say, 'Your sins are forgiven you, or to say, 'Arise and walk'? "But that you may know that the Son of Man has power on earth to forgive sins" – then He said to the paralytic, "Arise, take up your bed, and go to your house. "And he arose and departed to his house." Matt 9:4-7 Wow!

The Most Celebrated Birthday on Earth

Many have been born on earth. The population of the world is in billions. A great number have already passed away. Normally when people pass away, people cease to put much significance on their birthdays. Even some who could have had a lot of influence during their time on earth, people of the like of Martin Luther King,

Jesus Christ, 'Yesu' in Luganda

Jr. who took the words of Jesus very seriously, and brought about a civil change that benefited everybody in world, regardless of their creed or political orientation; people of the like of Martin Luther who let the world know that salvation, is by grace through faith in Jesus Christ, which impacted everybody on earth. Their birthdays are still celebrated, but only in a few places on the continents. In some places, especially the communities which they were not physically present, their birthday celebrations carry not much meaning, but But when it comes to Jesus Christ when it comes to Jesus Christ, it seems most people around the world find something in Him to celebrate; they are sending a message of appreciation for His birth into humanity. On the day of Christmas, more people have the opportunity to be with their families around the world. I saw it in China, America, Africa and Europe. Lights are lit everywhere, gifts are exchanged, songs are sung, even animals and birds notice the change in the attitude of the people, for they lean towards courtesy and goodness. No other person has this kind of a birthday that shakes up nations, cities, communities, lives; especially when it is done in His physical absence.

In most countries, Christmas is a federal holiday, every other thing is put on hold, to celebrate one who is none like any other – Jesus Christ, 'Yesu' in Luganda.

Unusual Events at the Birth of Jesus Christ-None Like It

The birth of Jesus Christ was very unusual. Records in the Bible indicate that His birth was prophesied long ago, before He came on the scene. His conception itself was sign to humanity. "Therefore, Behold the virgin shall conceive and bear a son, and shall call His name Immanuel." Is 7:14

Jesus was not conceived in the womb as other people on earth. He had no earthly father. At the time of His conception, Joseph the carpenter, was only betrothed to Mary. "Now the birth of Jesus Christ was as follows. After his mother Mary was betrothed to Joseph, before they came together, she was found with a child, by the Holy Spirit." Matt 1:18   There are many men and women who claim to be founders of various religions; but none of them say they were born without an earthly father. Even the Muslim Religion does not refute the virgin birth of Jesus Christ.

Adam was not born by a woman, God formed him out of the dust, and breathed into him the breath of life, and he became a living being, but Jesus was born by a woman, without the involvement of a man.

This by itself makes Jesus Christ stand out as 'peculiar' among all sons of men ever born, and this itself, puts Him in a very unique category – Divine. This event, attracted many of us to his person. We decided to hear as well as read what he had to say to us.

A Teacher Sent from God

There was a man of the Pharisees named Nicodemus, a ruler of the Jews. This man came to Jesus by night and said to Him, "Rabbi, we know that you are a teacher come from God, for no one could do these signs that you do unless God is with him." John 3:1-2. I totally agree with Nicodemus, on this matter. There are all kinds of teachers who have gone out to places and nations, some have caused major revolutions. They have lectured to nations very controversial theories regarding how to live and govern. But none of those people could heal a leper, raise the dead, remove demonic spells from people, through their many words.

These other teachers have no clearly recorded instances of divine acts, like the opening of blind eyes, as Jesus Christ did. There score in this aspect is 0%, but for Jesus it is 100%. Men like Marx, Lenin, Mao Se Tong, Gandhi, Buddha, Muhammad etc. Never even chased a single demon from anybody!!! "Now as Jesus

The Most Powerful People on Earth Revealed

Passed by, He saw a man who was blind from birth. And His disciples asked Him, saying, "Rabbi, who sinned, this man or his parents, that he was born blind!" Jesus answered, *"Neither this man nor his parents sinned, but that the works of God should be revealed in him. "I must work the works of Him who sent me while it is day; the night is coming when no one can work. 'As long as I am in the world, I am the light of the world.* "When He had said those things. He spat on the ground and made clay with the saliva; and He anointed the eyes of the blind man with the clay. And He said to him, *'Go wash in the pool of Siloam,'* (which is translated sent). So he went and washed, and came back seeing." John 9:1-7

I had to quote that entire Bible story, for some of you reading this book were told never to read the Bible. You have been restrained by some religious teachers from finding out who this Jesus Christ is. I was part of a big religious denomination before I became a born again Christian. That denomination I used to be part of then; they never let us read the Bible for ourselves, you only went by their rules and creed. Those were my early days of learning, whereby, we younger people were seeking knowledge for the betterment of our lives and others. We studied mathematics, chemistry, literature, history, geography, physics, commerce, biology, English, Luganda, French, accounting, typing, technical drawing, but we never studied the Bible.

I used to see some other church goers of the then Anglican Church in Uganda, now called Church of Uganda or Episcopal Church in America, carrying Bibles with them to church. So, I went to the priest at the Catholic Church, where I served as an altar boy, and asked him about it. This is what he told me. 'Those people do not trust their priests, that is why they search every word they say, if it is so in the Bible.'

Well, I said to him that in our classes at school, we are given text books to go along with the teachers teaching on that subject. He answered back, 'Not everyone is qualified to read the Bible. That book is only interpretable by Catholic priests.' That dialogue took place in the 1970's.

Get A Bible and Read It

Please get a Bible and read it, because you need to find out for yourself who this Jesus Christ is, and what makes Him stand out as the most loving individual who ever lived on earth.

You can't get to know Him and remain the same. You will find out that He is very likable: He is for you. "The thief does not come, except to steal, and to kill, and to destroy: I have come that they may have life and that they may have it more abundantly." John 10:10

An 87-year old, very influential Moslem Man turns to Jesus Christ before Passing Away

I was pastoring a church in Uganda, on the Eastern side of Kampala, then it was 1997. I did a lot of preaching and teaching in various churches in Africa, especially the Full Gospel churches. I was a born again, Spirit filled believer, followed by miracles, wonders and signs as I ministered. A confirmation of the Word of Jesus Christ to the believers in the book of Mark, "and these signs will follow those who believe, in my name they will cast out demons, they will speak with new tongues; they will take up serpents; and if they drink anything deadly, it will by no means hurt them; they will lay hands on the sick, and they will recover." Mark 16:17-18

Many people heard of the mighty things God was during through my life, even those who were in my neighborhood. This Moslem man happened to have a house, and land in the same village I lived in. His estate was next to my home of abode. Now, it had happened that he had fallen sick. This man had kindly given land to the Moslem faith to build a Mosque., and had also contributed financially to the Islamic faith in that region. He was held in high esteem by the people in that community.

The Man Battles with Sickness

What happened with this: he would come short of breath on his sick bed, and would convulse like dying, but never died. It was a very frightening incidence. Wherever it took place. He was hospitalized for some time, then they sent him home hoping he would be fine. However, that attack would come on him again, and again. Moslem Imams would come and pray all sorts of prayers for his recovery, but the sickness never went away, and they all became frustrated.

One of his daughters suggested that they invite this neighbor – a 'born-again' Christian pastor, to help, for she had heard that I pray for people in the Name of Jesus Christ, and they get healed, as well as receive their deliverance. This 87-year-old man, had a very big household. Six women were married to him, based on the Islamic faith.

Many of you may recall, that Idi Amin, a Moslem president, who ruled Uganda between 1971 and 1979, was married to various women, at the same time. He used to say that his faith allowed him and others to have as many wives as they can support. This man was of that kind of belief. He had many children and grandchildren.

I meet the man for the first time

I went to his house and I found him lying on his bed. He was surrounded by a lot of Moslem relatives. He said to me, 'Pastor, I have been having very bad nightmares, as well as evil encounters, in the last three recent attacks, I nearly died. I found myself in a very scary place with creatures that had shapes like human beings, but not really humans. Those creatures were mocking me as well as trying to grab me.

They were trying to drag me into a very dark place, where I could hear wailings, weeping, and great anguish. This happened three times. I barely survived. Please, can you help me?'

Those around his bed said that they could see him struggling, like he was wrestling an invisible enemy, which was trying to take life out of him. They said that they have done everything they know to do to help him, they even put a Koran – the book of the Muslim Faith, on his chest hoping that some supernatural power would manifest, to the help of this man, but all that was in vain; it never brought him peace. They had even consulted a sorcerer to come and ease this man's agony, but that never worked either. This had been going on for three months. The most recent time this man had a convulsion, they thought he had died, but he came back to life, talking and screaming, 'leave me alone, I don't like you and I don't know you!'

I Introduced the Man to Jesus Christ

I opened the Holy Bible, for this man had asked me a question, 'Where is Heaven? How come when I was dying, I did not see heaven, all I saw were demons.' I told him that he has to know, as well as receive in his life the most powerful being on earth, who conquered Death-Jesus Christ.

He let me know that, in his religion, Jesus Christ, was made known to him by the teachings of Islam as a great prophet. I said to him, that is also right, but He is more than a prophet; He is the Son of the Living God, and He lives today, among us. "I am He who lives, and was dead, and behold, I am alive forevermore. Amen. And I have the keys of Hades and of Death." Rev 1:18

I also introduced him to John 3:16, "For God so loved the world that He gave His only begotten Son,

That whoever believes in Him should not perish but have everlasting life. "For God did not send His Son into the world to condemn the world, but that the world through Him might be saved." John 3:16-17

This man had a very inquisitive mind, he reminds me of the people of Berea, whom the Bible describes as fair minded people, who gave Paul the opportunity to share with them the Gospel – good news. These people, the Bible says, received the word of God with all readiness and searched the scriptures daily to find out whether these things were so. You can find this narrative in the book of Acts Chapter Seventeen from verse ten to verse twelve.

This precious 87-year-old man had never heard those words read to him before. The Islam religion that he was brought up in by his parents, gave him a book, which was not the Bible, but it is called, a Koran. It does not say much about Jesus Christ. All that he knew was that Jesus Christ was born by a virgin woman, Mary or Maria of course the same person, but different languages. To my amazement He was also taught that Jesus never died on the cross, but He was snatched away by God and somebody else died in His stead. He had also been told, that, Prophet Jesus Christ will come back to judge the living and the dead. The fact that He had been in Hell, even though He prayed three times every day, in the Islamic faith, right on his knees as an act of reverence to God and had bowed to the ground many times facing Mecca, made him question the soundness of his faith; especially since weird creatures could still have access to his soul. That moved him to reevaluate his stakes. He really had a lot of questions for me, and that was alright with me; that is what pastors are for.

I really do not want to be misunderstood concerning this very powerful book I am writing. The testimonies like this one, are factual incidences that took place, and I am narrating them the way they happened, exactly. I love God's people and mostly, I love God, so I would not do anything to hurt you. I am just a messenger of truth.

This man was ready for the truth, and the truth only. He said he does not care about religions any more, what he wanted is to be sure he will go to heaven when he dies.

Jesus Christ the only way, truth and life

I did not have to spend much time to convince this dear elderly precious man, that what he has trusted in since birth, was not working. What he needed was something real, that works. In my family, we owned an automobile repair shop, my uncle a brother to my mother, was very gifted in engineering. He had this company called, 'Buddu Engineering Works.' During some of my school holidays, I would go and work with him in his automobile repair shop. He was really very good at fixing cars, that was his specialty. He did work for the Catholic Archdiocese of Kampala, the Cooperative Bank and other large institutions.

One thing that caught my attention was the fact that the customers would come in and say, 'Do you believe that you can fix this vehicle for us? We took it to so and so, but the vehicle is still faulty.' Then he would tell them, 'I can fix it, and I do fix these kinds of cars. I went to school and graduated with high honors. This problem is no match to me,' and sure enough, we did fix their vehicles, and they left extremely happy.

This elderly man rightly deserved a good answer concerning his life. I quoted another important scripture to him from the Bible. "Thomas said to Him, "Lord, we do not know where you are going and how can we know the way?" Jesus said to him, "I am the Way, the truth and the life. No one comes to the Father except through Me." John 14:6 When I was reading the Word of God to this man, I saw his eyes open widely, his expression was like, 'Oh my God, I did not know that!' Then he said, 'Preacher, how do I become part of Jesus Christ?'

Point to Note: Religion is something put on you – that is not what you are.

There are people today, when you ask them what is your faith, they say I am a Mormon; Moslem; Hindu; Catholic; Jehovah Witness; Methodist; Presbyterian; Baptist; etc. The way how people take on these kind of identities, is sometimes scary, for some use them to kill, hate, as well as to cause discord among humanity, especially when people take a none-love attitude.

The Nazis in Germany used their identity to exploit, murder, steal as well as inflict destruction to everything in their sight. Even animals and birds in the air felt their wickedness. It was sickening. Those labels put on you by religions and various ideologies are not what you are. You are a human being, created in the image of God. "Then God said, "Let us make man in our image, according to our likeness; let them have dominion over the fish of the sea, over the birds of the air, over the cattle, over all creeping things that creep on the earth, "So God created man in His own image. In the image of God. He created him, male and female He created them." Gen 1:26-27 Your true identify is found in God. Do not let the tag put on you by human beings or human institutions dictate the direction of your life. Jesus said in the Gospel of Matthew, in the Holy Bible, that the most important two commandments are: "Jesus said to him, "You shall love the LORD your God with all your heart, with all your soul, with all your mind. "This is the first and great commandment. "And the second is like it, 'You shall love your neighbor as yourself." "On these two commandments hang all the law and the prophets." Matt 22:37-40

The 87 year-old Moslem man receives Jesus Christ as His Personal Savior

This man told me he was willing to come to Christ. When I was ministering to him, I made sure I treated him fairly. I saw him as any other human being who needed salvation I made sure that the label of "religion" on him does not stand in the way of our interaction. I lead him through the Prayer of Salvation, "that, if you confess with your mouth the Lord Jesus, and believe in your heart, that God has raised Him, from the dead, you will be saved." Rom 10:9 He did that, and I declared him a 'born-again' believer, according to Second Corinthians Chapter Five, Verse Seventeen, "Therefore, if anyone is in Christ, he is a new creation

Jesus Christ, 'Yesu' in Luganda

Old things have passed away, behold all things have become new." 2 Cor 5:17 You could see a change on his face right there; his countenance lighted up. I could see a glean in his eyes. He asked me so many questions about Jesus Christ. He wanted to know so much about Him. I took some time and read to him the Gospel of John in the Holy Bible. He was fascinated about his person.

Jesus Christ is a Lovable Person

Jesus is not a religion: He is the Son of God, loveable, kind, compassionate, gentle, divine. We need to know His person, and the place to learn about Him is, the Holy Bible, and churches that are Christ centered. Churches where Jesus Christ is recognized as both Lord and Savior. Beloved, Jesus rose from the dead, that distinguishes Him, from all other founders of religions as well as teachers.

I had to share this with you, in case through this book you are having your first deeper understanding of who the savior is. The 87-year-old man told me that, if he had somebody to explain to him the way of the Lord long ago when he was still young, he would have become a Christian then. He said to me, "I only knew

Him as a Holy Prophet, and not as a Savior, but now I am glad that He is my Lord and Savior. Today I confess that Jesus Christ died and rose from the dead, and I am a born again Christian. All his relatives who were in that room, on that day, were perplexed, but because they held him in great respect, none dared argue with him.

The Old Man Passes Away after Three Weeks

From the time that man received Jesus Christ as his personal Savior, everything changed about him. He stopped having nightmares, those around him noticed that peace beyond understanding had embraced him. He was no longer thinking about death, but heaven. When I went to visit him the next week, he asked me so many questions about heaven.

I shared with him from the scriptures, the beauty of heaven, and how Jesus Christ has even mansions for us, prepared by God, our Father. "Let not your heart be troubled. You believe in God, believe also in me. "In My Father's house are many mansions, if it were not so, I would have told you. I go to prepare a place for you." "And if I go and prepare a place for you. I will come again and receive you to myself that where I am, there you may be also. And where I go, you know and the

Way you know," John 14:1-4 This man liked that scripture; he even had it written on a paper in big words for him to meditate on. After three weeks, my friend passed on peacefully. Just that made a believer out of all who saw his passing away. They said that he was resting on his bed when they realized he had passed on. There was a childlike smile on his face.

I saw his body; his demeanor was of someone who had transitioned in peace. Being a pastor and a bishop, I happen to perform quite a number of funerals and I do view the bodies of the deceased. Sometimes, I can tell by looking at the face and posture of the body, how the going to the other place of abode was.

A Human Being is not Just a Body

I would like to pause a little bit here, and teach. A human being is a spirit with a soul, living in a body. When people die, the spirit comes out of the body and transits to a place, it can be either Hell or Heaven. When you look in the book of Genesis, Chapter Four, around verse number eight, the Word of God declares, "Now Cain talked with Abel his brother, and it came to pass, when they were in the field, that Cain rose up against Abel his brother and killed him." Gen 4:8 This is the first act of murder recorded in the Holy Bible. It is very possible that Cain thought he would get away with that murder, on the assumption that man is just a body. To his surprise, God let him know that there is a part in Abel his brother, which he was not able to kill, and that was still speaking. "Then the LORD said to Cain, "Where is Abel your brother?" He said, "I do not know. Am I my brother's keeper?" And He said, "What have you done? The voice of your brother's blood cries out to Me from the ground. So now you are cursed from the earth, which has opened its mouth to receive your brother's blood from your hand." Gen 4:9-11.

Some people do bad things to others with a belief that when people die, that is the end of them. Of course, that is not true. Those people, though they are dead in the natural, but their spirits are still intact. They can talk to God and God can talk to them. We see this in the book of Revelation as well, of those who were martyred because of their faith. "When He opened the fifth seal, I saw under the altar the souls of those who had been slain for the word of God and for the testimony which they held. And they cried with a loud voice, saying, "How long, O Lord, holy and true, until

Jesus Christ, 'Yesu' in Luganda

You judge and avenge our blood on those who dwell on the earth?" Then a white robe was given to each of them; and it was said to them that they should rest a little while longer, until both the number of their fellow servants and their brethren, who would be killed as they were, was completed." Rev 6:9-11

In this scripture, it is evident that when a person passes away from this life, their souls which can be interchangeable for their spirit, to break it down the soul of a human being, is that part of the spirit that enables that person to hear, speak, see, and feel, etc. That is why when a person goes to Hell, they can experience the burning and all other kinds of pain, and what is amazing, they don't die again from that fire. Those who go to Heaven also experience the beauty and the rest they are in, and they can intelligently communicate their case.

In Uganda, the nation in which I was born, there are some 45 Saints who were martyred because of their faith in our Lord Jesus Christ. These simple men, who possibly would not have been known about, and whose names would be nowhere in important books; today they attract millions of people from all walks of life, across nations who come to celebrate their act of bravery and sacrifice, over 4 million people showed up

The Most Powerful People on Earth Revealed

To worship God at the site, in 2018. These people are one of the big reasons why we have education and civilization in Africa. They embraced the Words of our Lord Jesus Christ, honored God, up to their final breath. Some were burned at stake with fire, others were speared through the heart, so many cruel things were done to these people, but I really believe, that today they are alive and well in God the Father's Kingdom.

As an historian, and an anointed writer, I have made some observation about those who killed them and their linages. It seems that very bad consequences befell upon them, things have happened and did happen to those people and their lineages, which only the blood of Jesus Christ can remove. There is no atonement without the shedding of blood. It is only through the atonement on the cross of Jesus Christ that judgment can be held away from those who transgress, the Word of God – thou shall not shed innocent blood.

Contend for your Soul

Beloved, you have to contend for your soul. Life here on earth ends. You are going to spend eternity somewhere. That is why you must make sure, like this 87-year-old man, that you are on the right path. Do not let anyone, lie to you that you are just a body; NO, NO, you are a spirit, with a soul, living in a body. It is within your power to decide where you are going to spend eternity. God has sent pastors, prophets, evangelists, teachers, apostles and so many other gifts to help us make the right decisions about our destiny. God loves all of us.

The 87 year-old Former Moslem Man Wills that: I, a born-again Christian pastor, preside over His Funeral!

As you are very well aware, through the testimony of this man's conversation, he was a Moslem for so many years and had invested his life and money into that religion. But, when he came to know Jesus Christ, three weeks before his death, he found in Him a Savior and friend. He became a disciple of Jesus Christ, and a 'born again' Christian.

The major concern now was, how he was going to be buried, who was to preside over his funeral and where to bury him. Well, the wise man had already resolved that. He had instructed his estate lawyer to document this, 'My funeral in case I pass away eventually, shall be presided over by the pastor; Bishop Leonard Kayiwa of Christian Faith Center, Kamyokya, Kampala. He shall do all the duties of a Christian pastor in regard to my funeral and burial, for I received Jesus Christ as my personal savior.'

That was very strong, beloved of God. Heavenly act.

I started meetings with his family for burial preparations. The Sheikhs of the Moslem religion started talking to me, they were perplexed and a little bit confused, not sure if this was really the man who had been with them for a long time. Well, they were right. It was not the old man any more, the man had become a new creation, "Therefore, if anyone is in Christ, he is a new creation; old things have passed away; behold, all things have become new." 2 Cor 5:17

This man was regarded by most of them, as a decent, honorable, generous person. One deserving to be celebrated for the many acts of love he had performed in their community. Others were puzzled, wondering what caused him to change his heart in regard to religion. There is one thing they could not argue about, the fact that he was mature and that he might have made the right decision.

Preaching to a Congregation where 96% were Moslems

The funeral was organized at one of the large properties he owned. Tents were set up there, it was a large open space with two buildings on the site. There were so many people of the Moslem faith in attendance, and few from other faiths. I went to the funeral with four other pastors, and our worship team. It was a sunny day. I could hear Moslems greeting one another in Arabic. The casket was right there for everyone to view. He was eulogized by various friends and family members. Eventually a Shaikh from the mosque where he used to go for prayer most of his life, and which the deceased had invested in financially, stood up and asked for the attention of the people, and this is what he said, 'Brethren, our beloved Father, Friend, Grandfather, Husband, who has departed from us, willed that Pastor Leonard Kayiwa preside over his funeral, and in respect for his wishes, I do hereby invite the pastor to the podium to guide as well as officiate this funeral.'

When he said that, there was a deep silence of disbelief and wonder among those Moslems. They did not know what to expect.

I Teach About the Truth of God's Word, and Many Are Touched

Please go with me in the sermon the Lord God gave me that day, for His precious people, during that very decisive funeral in Mitiyana, not very far from the capital city of Uganda in Africa: -

Ladies and gentlemen, you all know why we are here; the parent, friend and associate is no longer with us. He has passed on. What we have amidst us is his body. The casket is visibly in our midst. Death has had

-143-

a toll on us, and elsewhere, all over the world. This event is always a tragedy that raises many questions, and which cannot be ignored.

How did we get here?

Man was created in the image of God, and was given dominion over the works of God, according to the Word of God in the Holy Bible, written by Prophet Moses in the book of Genesis, Chapter One, verse twenty-six. "Then God said, "Let Us make man in Our image, according to Our likeness, let them have dominion over the fish..." Gen 1:26

Just gleaning through that Word of God, you come face to face with the fact that there has to be more than one being in the person of God, or He would not have said, 'Let Us'. That 'Us' indicates a pluralism in the Godhead, but I would rather get on to the second point that applies directly to this situation we are dealing with; a dead among us. "And the LORD God commanded the man, saying, "Of every tree of the garden you may freely eat; but the tree of the Knowledge of Good and Evil you shall not eat, for the day that you eat of it you shall surely die." Gen 2:16-17

This Word, command was given to man at his creation, when God entrusted him with a piece of real estate, to live in as well as attend to it. But man was lied to by the enemy of his soul, Satan – the old serpent.

Jesus Christ, 'Yesu' in Luganda

The devil in the form of a serpent, appeared in the Garden of Eden, and told the woman these words. "Then the Serpent Said to the woman, "You will not surely die. "For God knows that in the day you eat of it your eyes will be opened and you will be like God, knowing good and evil." Gen 3:4-5 Ladies and gentlemen, we have one of our own lying here dead, due to a lie by Satan disguising itself as an angel of light.

Because of one act of the disobedience of man, all people of all creeds, nationality, status, or religion everywhere on earth, are being infested by this tragedy of death.

We need the truth.

When I arrived to this point of my sermon, I noticed that all eyes were widely open upon me. You could hear a pin drop. The level of attention they gave those words was amazing. I was teaching, not just preaching. They were my audience. Just looking into their eyes, I could determine that they understood very well what God had given me to share with them.

Many of these congregants had Muslim hats on their heads, women were wearing a head covering, according to the traditions of Islam. These people were ripe for the truth. The undisputable evidence of the consequences of disobedience were right before them, the body of my friend; the 87-year-old, Christian man had left behind, a lifeless body: A consequence of a lie to humanity by the liar-the Devil. This what our Lord Jesus Christ said about this liar, "The thief does not come except to steal and to kill, and to destroy. I have come that they may have life, and that they may have it more abundantly." John 10:10

Adam and Eve lost the estate God had prepared for them, and lived a life of toiling, which was never the origin intent of God; and sadly, they had to die. That is why you cannot afford to build your life on a lie.

Jesus Christ – The Truth

The only man, person, whoever took the truth very seriously, that we know and have records of in regard to this very important subject is: Jesus Christ. He said of Himself, "Jesus said to him. "I am the Way, the truth and the life. No one comes to the Father except through me." John 14:6 I let those people, right there at the funeral to consider the situation in which that man was in. He sought to do no harm to anyone; but he was just in pursuit of God and the truth; especially since He knew that His time on earth was coming to an end. Precious people of God, I believe it is reasonable to conclude that the most important concern he had before he passed, was to know the truth regarding what would happen to him after death.

Jesus Christ, 'Yesu' in Luganda

Pilate at the Trial of Jesus Christ, became very interested in knowing the truth and asked a number of questions. "Are you a king, then?" Jesus answered, "I am a king, for this cause I was born, and for this cause I have come into the world, that I should bear witness to the truth. Everyone who is of the truth hears my words." John 10:37   Pilate is trying his best to resolve the conflict the Jewish leaders had against Jesus Christ, concerning His teachings.

Some people treasured the teachings of Jesus Christ, but others took offense at His words. The Prophet Jesus was such a challenge to them, that they would rather see Him dead then abandoning their vile lifestyles. Pilate knew that Jesus had done nothing deserving death. He had perceived that the battle was about the truth; "Pilate Said to Him, 'What is truth?' And when He had said this, he went out again to the Jews, and Said to them, 'I find no fault in Him at all.' John 18:38

The man who converted and became a follower of Jesus Christ, made his judgment in regard to the truth and concluded that Jesus Christ was not only telling the truth, but He is the Truth. This man whose funeral I was presiding at, fell in love with the person of Jesus Christ. He understood, at the time of his death, that what matters beyond death is the truth. You don't want to find yourself where you believed a lie and end up in

Hell. Adam and Eve believed a lie and brought all humanity to the tragedy of death and toil, "In the sweat of your face you shall eat bread. Till you return to the ground, for out of it you were taken; For dust you are, And to dust you shall return." Gen 3:19

God the Father, God the Son and God the Holy Spirit are one, and in God there is no darkness. "If we say that we have fellowship with Him, and walk in darkness, we lie and do not practice the truth. But if we walk in the light as He is in the light, we have fellowship with one another, and the blood of Jesus Christ His Son cleanses us from all sin. If we say that we have no sin, we deceive ourselves and the truth is not in us. If we confess our sins, He is faithful and just to forgive us of sins and to cleans us from all unrighteousness." 1 John 1:6-9

You who is reading this book in case you are not yet converted to Christianity; that is received Jesus Christ as your personal savior, it is time to do so now. God has lead me to share with you this amazing testimony. A good number of those who attended that funeral ended up becoming, 'born again' Christians. They received Jesus Christ as their Lord and Savior. They left the places they had been going to, to attend prayers and started attending the Spirit filled Christian churches. Some joined the church I was pastoring.

The worship songs that day during the funeral, by our church choir, were amazing. Those people gave glory to God. This man's home going was glorious. I let them know that our friend and brother was in Heaven with Jesus Christ, for the Holy Scriptures make it very, very clear, that for a believer to be absent from the body, is to be present with the Lord. "For we walk by faith, not by sight. We are confident, yes, well pleased rather to be absent from the body and to be present with the Lord." 2 Cor 5:7-8

Jesus Christ – The Demon Crusher (Destroyer)

In the opening scripture of this Title – that is, Chapter Three, the Word of God brings us to a scenery whereby Jesus Christ was teaching in a synagogue. This is in the book of Mark, Chapter One. It was a Sabbath, and worshippers were gathered as usual to hear the Word of God ministered by the Rabbis. I would rightly say that those people had already had an opportunity to learn from various teachers.

That day, they encountered something unusual, "Now there was a man in their synagogue, with an unclean spirit. And he cried out saying, "Let us alone! What have we to do with you Jesus of Nazareth? Did you come to destroy us? I know who you are – the Holy One of God!" Mark 1: 23-24 Just His Holy presence disturbed evil. In this situation it is apparent that the wicked spirits that day could not abode comfortably in their captive; that person in whom they were not supposed to be. These evil spirits were transgressing. For man was made in the image of God, and in His likeness, not to be a house of demons.

Possibly these devils would sit comfortably in this individual when other teachers were teaching at the synagogue, for these teachers lacked the power to challenge them.   But, that day when the demon destroyer – Jesus Christ came into the synagogue and taught, those spirits were arrested, they felt the Holy Presence of God, tormenting them.

Jesus was teaching when they interrupted His sermon. I know some of you are saying, 'I don't see these kinds of things happening in my place of worship'. Well, for that to happen, there has to be 'power' or 'authority' superior to theirs. Otherwise, as long as they are unchallenged, they can easily come into a synagogue or church building or a Mosque building, etc., within individuals and leave with them uncontested, for it takes power to chase them out.

"But Jesus rebuked him, saying, 'Be quiet, and come out of him!" And when the unclean spirit had convulsed him and cried out with a loud voice he came out of him." Mark 1:25-26   This devil was punished. It was forcefully halted from residing in him;

rebuked, tormented, and uprooted from this person, because of Jesus Christ. These acts of amazing authority and power makes Him the most powerful individual who ever lived on earth.

Those in that synagogue, were all amazed; they said, 'What is this? What new doctrine is this, for with authority, He commands even the unclean spirits, And they obey Him.' That is why you need to know Jesus Christ, for your protection, for there are nasty spirits out there called devils and demons.

Jesus Christ – the storm rebuker

The journey of life is like traveling in a boat on the sea, and having to face all sorts of storms and winds contrary to your direction, waves as well as a lot of uncertainty. The visible and invisible players are all part of the equation. You need someone in your boat with supernatural authority; that can change the course of the torrents, in case it is working against you.

There is a situation in the Bible which I would like to bring to your attention, this is in the book of Mark, Chapter Four, "On the same day, when evening had come, He said to them, "Let us cross over to the other side." Now, when they had left the multitude, they took Him along in the boat as He was. And other little boats were also with Him. And a great windstorm arose and the waves beat into the boat, so that it was already fill-ing. But he was in the stern, asleep on a pillow. And they awake Him and said to Him, "Teacher, do you not care that we are perishing." Then He arose and rebuked the wind and said to the sea, "Peace, be still." And the wind ceased and there was a great calm. But He said to them, "Why are you so fearful? How is it that you have no faith?" And they feared exceedingly, and said to one another, 'Who can this be, that even the wind and the sea obey Him!" Mark 4:35-41

Winds and the sea obey Him; one who speaks to the elements and they heed His voice; He is being introduced to you in this very spectacular encounter. He did not have an electrical remote control gudget in His hands; this is not electrical power, fire power, human power, but something else, for He only said a word and it was done. Precious ones, He is still the same yesterday, today and forever. "Jesus Christ is the same yesterday, today, and forever." Heb 13:8. I am so glad that I know Him, especially that I received Him as my Lord and Savior. He is my friend.

Jesus Christ – the Resurrection

Death has taken toll on all human beings. Cemeteries are everywhere, I have seen them in Africa, Asia, America, Europe, etc. Nearly all men have this in common – they die at a certain time. I have known many that I attended school with, which, as I write this

Jesus Christ, 'Yesu' in Luganda

Book today in 2018, they are already buried. Those who never even gave much thought to the fact that death is a reality, and in their lifetime, never considered what would be next in case it happens.

Jesus Christ, of all sons of men, who ever lived, addressed this phenomenon of death in a very hopeful way. He had more understanding of it than any other philosopher, teacher, Rabbi, or prophet who ever lived on this earth. People have so many theories about this matter, and when you examine them closely, they are just myths.

Some say, when a person dies, that is the end of them. Others think or believe that people come back to exist after death in form of other creations. To some, death completely silences everything.

A Man Tells People at a State Funeral Something Very Awkward Concerning Life after Death

There was a government funeral in a certain nation. The man who had died was a high ranking officer in the police force. So many had gathered to the burial ground to put away his remains. The entire service was televised and streamed all over the world. A number of eulogist were summoned to the podium to say something. One of them was a retired army general.

This man really seemed to have had a great respect and honor for the deceased than most people at the burial ground. He knew the man who had passed, very well. He had worked along with him for many years. When he was given the microphone, he consoled the mourners by telling them that the good news is, because the deceased man was a good man, most likely he will re-incarnate as a nice animal or a good insect, or possibly a very good looking bird!

He really did not have substance to back his theory, but he seemed to believe what he was saying. He is not the only one who believes this way. There are so many of them out there. To them, life after death is a big mystery. Well, my recommendation to any one concerning the mystery of death, is to read the teachings of Jesus Christ.

Jesus Proves to be the True Authority to Address Death and Resurrection

In the book of John of the Gospel in the Holy Bible, words are recorded concerning a very breath catching event involving Jesus Christ. A man by the name of Lazarus of Bethany, fell sick and eventually died. He was a friend of Jesus, he and his family knew the Lord, Jesus Christ.

The funeral took place in the absence of Jesus Christ. Many came to console the family. His body was placed in a tomb and a big stone was rolled over the entrance. Many teachers of the law then; the Pharisees and

Jesus Christ, 'Yesu' in Luganda

Sadducees, attended the burial ceremony, and a good number of Jews had joined the sisters of Lazarus; Martha and Mary to comfort them concerning their brother; for death had struck one of their very own. Grief was everywhere, until Jesus Christ arrived.

"Now Martha said to Jesus, "Lord if you had been here my brother would not have died." John 11:21 Martha had the opportunity to see miracles done by our Lord Jesus Christ. She had very possibly witnessed the numerous people having been healed through the compassion of Jesus. No wonder she could with very great confidence say that, if Jesus was with them at the time of sickness of their brother, he would have healed him.

But now, they are dealing with death. That one which most teachers of the law could not turn around. All they could offer was eulogies and 'from dust you came, to dust your return.'

The Bible points out, that on that day many saw another side of Jesus they had never beheld until then. They realized that this man cannot just be a mere man, there is something divine about Him. "Jesus said to her, "I am the resurrection and the life. He who believes in Me though he may die, he shall live. "And whoever lives and believes in me shall never die. Do you believe this?" John 11:25-26.

The Most Powerful People on Earth Revealed

Going to school in Uganda, Africa, two of the subjects that fascinated me were mathematics, and physics. I loved studying mathematics, I would solve very tricky equations. To me, mathematics is like another world full of adventure. God blessed me with understanding of this subject. My fellow students at St. Henry's College, Kitovu, Masaka recognized that.

They would come to me for help in that subject, they thought I was a mathematical genius, even the teachers would tell my fellow students that 'you can go to him for help to solve mathematical problems you are facing,' Though I was a student at that college, I ended up becoming a teacher unofficially to many of my fellow students, and I did it with gladness. I also found out that the more I helped my friends, the better mathematician I became.

Let me teach a little bit on this matter.

It is very, very important to be generous with the gifts God has given you, those gifts were put in your life for the benefit of all. Sometimes, people have a lot of resources, and wonder why they have so much, while others have so little. I would like you to understand this. Everything we have, we are just stewards. "The earth is the LORD's and all its fullness, The world and those who dwell therein. For He has founded it upon the seas, And established it upon the waters." Ps 24:1-2 God owns ever thing, all the money belongs to Him, and every good and perfect gift comes from Him. We need to be willing to distribute, share, apply, communicate, teach, share the cures, as well as bring a good change in the lives of people through what God has entrusted us with. The more we give, the more He gives to us, "Give, and it will be given to you: good measure, pressed down, shaken together, and running over will be put into your bosom. For with the same measure that you use, it will be measured back to you." Luke 6:38

This book you are reading today, would not have been possible if it was not for the generosity of the believers. Normally I tell people that when you send me a monetary seed of at least $25, we send you a copy of this book. What actually I am saying is, let us share what God has given us to benefit others; amazing enough, some individuals have honored this, and have even given more than twenty dollars to make this ministry of the written word possible.

People have been healed by reading my books. I wrote a book entitled, 'Receive your Healing in the Name of Jesus Christ of Nazareth.' Testimonies upon testimonies of deliverance and healing have been reported to us, by God's people, that God confirmed His Word in their lives in regard to healing. Precious people of God, it is all about being good stewards of what God has placed in your life. Each one of us has something God put in you for the benefit of His creation. The Bible says, "Therefore He says: "When He ascended on high, He led captivity captive, And gave gifts to men." Eph 4:8 The scripture is referring to Jesus Christ.

Some of the fellow students that I helped in mathematics and physics today they have obtained Ph.D's in different trades, and are benefitting the world. Others have taken on different trades, to the benefit of the communities where they live. Dare to share the gifts God has put in your life, and you will reap the benefits of it.

Regarding mathematics, you don't just go ahead and write or say things, you need to prove in detail the point you are trying to make. Physics also falls in the same category, these two subjects, along with Chemistry could be the real force behind modernization. The three figure combination I did before joining the university was: Mathematics (both Pure and Applied); Physics; and Chemistry. The other two hinges on mathematics.

Coming from that background, of those three disciplines, you don't walk up to me and claim things without proof, you have to prove what you are saying, for me to believe you. In regard to the resurrection, the Bible says, Jesus came to the tomb and asked them to take away the stone. This tomb was a cave, and a stone lay against it. This man had died already; four days in the tomb. They did not have enough Chemistry, Physics and Mathematics in combination with Biology to preserve the body. He was already stinking, for his body was decomposing.

Jesus Resurrects the Dead Man!!!

They took away the stone at the command of Jesus Christ. "Take away the stone." Martha, the sister of him who was dead, said to him, "Lord by this time there is a stench, for he has been dead four days." John 11:38-39

The preceding verses regarding this event at the tomb of Lazarus unveils the deity of Jesus Christ, "Now when He had said these things. He cried with a loud voice, "Lazarus come forth." And he who died came out bound hand and foot with grave clothes, and his face was wrapped with a cloth. Jesus said to them, "Loose him and let him go." Then many of the Jews who had come to Mary, and had seen the things Jesus did, believed in Him." John 11:43-45

Precious one, who is reading this book, I do hereby submit to you that the most powerful man who ever lived on earth, is Jesus Christ: This man conquered death. This is the one you need to follow; read about and to know personally.

Jesus Christ – the Changer of Lives

I knew some people way back when we were young boys attending school, and some of them were busy bodies; those that would try to get into everyone else's business. Naughty people, who seemed to feed on trouble making, I mean bullies; very unreasonable persons, whom you would not even want to be around.

These boys found pleasure in teasing other students. I saw a lot of that when I was at St. Henry's College, Kitovu, Masaka, in Uganda, Africa. This institution was founded by Catholic brothers. It occupied a very nice hill, with very nice buildings, with very nice facilities to help produce stellar students and God fearing people.

There was a chapel at that college, where church services were conducted every day, in the morning and in the evening. By the time I joined that college, the Ugandan government had become the biggest stake holder, providing maintenance, teachers, supplies, as well as the curriculum. The school was under the ministry of education

There were all kinds of rules put in place back then, to try to keep everyone safe and healthy, as well as to prevent bullies from having their way. There were some students who just could not get it. No wonder the Bible says, all have sinned and they need a savior. "For all have sinned and fall short of the glory of God being justified freely by His grace through the redemption that is in Christ Jesus." Rom 3:23-24

A Very Nasty Boy then Turns into a Very Decent Man

This boy was nasty, very violent at school, always trying bad tricks on others, and very loud. Most of the other students, did not want to be around him. He would sometimes pour water on their beds at night; St. Henry's College was a boarding school, we stayed in dormitories. The motto of that college was, 'For Greater Horizons', but this particular student was opposite of all decency.

He was suspended a number of times, but out of the grace of those Christian brothers, he was allowed to return. To make it worse, some other students joined him who thought he was a great person. He narrowly escaped going to jail and being hatched down by those whom he abused. You could easily come to the conclusion that he would not live long.

We left the college, and continued our education to various universities. I did not hear about him for almost six years.

The Boy Ends Up Becoming a Magistrate

One of the friends I was at college with, was narrating some of the wonders he had observed, and he said to me, 'Do you remember so and so, that very bad boy at the college we attended?' I said, 'yes.' 'Well, he is still alive and he did law and became a judge. Something unusual must have happened to him.' My friend said, 'this boy, there is no way he could become a magistrate, unless he knew someone.'

When I heard this, I made it my intension to find out what had happened. I called his office in that particular city in Uganda. It was a circuit court. I left my contact information for the judge, with the court clerk, hoping that he would call me back.

He did call me back. I was pastoring a church at that time, in Kamwokya 'Christian Faith Center,' he said, Pastor, I am so glad to hear from you. Jesus is amazing! You are now a preacher? We thought you were destined to just be an engineer or a great academician.

Jesus Christ is awesome. Just hearing that was enough for me to understand that this man who was never expected to amount to anything, was now settling disputes between people at the court – he was a judge.

He let me know, that he had met Jesus Christ, the Son of the Living God, and Jesus Christ had changed his life, set him free from bad habits and influences, and gave him a new life. He said he has a godly family, and God has made him a better and successful person; that Jesus Christ, set him free. "Therefore, if the Son makes you free, you shall be free indeed." John 8:36

Jesus Christ, 'Yesu' in Luganda

I knew him, he could never sit down and concentrate on his studies. He used to come to me for help, he was that kind of student who would 'copy' during exams. Very few people believed in him. They thought that his life would be cut off at any time, due to his wickedness.

He met Jesus Christ

He explained to me how he met a group of missionaries from the United States of America, in his early manhood. They prayed for him, and also introduced Jesus to him, as a savior. He said those people had power: 'When they prayed for me, something electrical like went through my whole body and something bad left me: anger, filthiness, vileness, confusion, and hopelessness.'

'I knew I had become a new person, a desire to be a good person came into my life. I stopped looking at people with suspicion, but love, and I picked up interest to read books and excel in my studies. Everything changed around me. It was like, I became a new creation.' Well, this is in line with the words in the Holy Bible, *"Therefore, if anyone is in Christ, he is a new creation. Old things have passed away, behold all things have become new." 2 Cor 5:17*

You Can Also Change

In case you are reading this book and you know you need to be a better person; husband, wife, student, child

Worker, governor, president, physician. A person who brings joy, peace righteousness, to any other person you happen to be near. The recommendation for you is Jesus Christ, the Son of the living God. Receive Him as your personal savior and you shall be saved. 'For the Scripture says, "Whoever believes in Him will not be put to shame." For there is no distinction between Jew and Greeks, for the same Lord over all is rich to all who call upon Him." Rom 10:11-12 Know that Jesus Christ is the most powerful person who ever lived on earth.

Jesus Christ – Conquered Death

Men and women have come to the world, born to various families and people. Some have had very sad impact on humanity. All that they are known for is the suffering they caused, especially killings and murder. There are those who never brought to humanity any particular remedy to the enemy, death, but only became agents of death. Later, they became victims of the same as those they brutally mistreated and took away their dreams and lives.

Ultimately, what they left behind, were white bones, lying in their infamous tombs. Jesus called them white washed tombs, full of dead men's bones – death conquered them. What is amazing about these infamous people whose names are not fit to be mentioned in this powerful book, they lived like they would never die; they lived in denial. The Bible says, Jesus died also: He gave up His Spirit publicly at the cross, with so many watching. 'So when Jesus had received the sour wine, He said, "It is finished!" And bowing His head, He gave up His spirit." John 19:30

Please, do not let anyone lie to you that Jesus Christ was snatched away and someone else was crucified in His place. That is not true, that teaching is false. If you want to know what happened at Golgotha, you have to read the Bible. The Holy Bible is the infallible Word of God: That is where you will find the truth, and that truth will set you free. "And you shall know the truth, and the truth shall make you free." John 8:32

The Pharisees did not want to hear anything else, except what they already heard. They were not willing to be progressive, when they heard the scripture I have just quoted, they answered Him. "We are Abraham's descendants, and have never been in bondage to anyone. How can you say you will be made free?" Jesus answered them, "Most assuredly say to you, whoever commits sin is a slave of sin." John 8:33-34

When Jesus came to the world, He willingly decided to take on sin. The Bible says, He became sin for us that we might become the righteousness of God. He had to die, for the wages of sin is death. What was different about Him from any other person on earth, is the fact that no one had power to take His life. He willingly laid down His life through the horrifying suffering at the cross. He was buried in a borrowed tomb, "Now when evening had come, there came a rich man from Arimathea, named Joseph, who himself had also become a disciple of Jesus. This man went to Pilate and asked for the body of Jesus. Then Pilate commanded the body to be given to him. When Joseph had taken the body, he wrapped it in a clean linen cloth, and laid it in his new tomb, which he had hewn out of the rock; and he rolled a large stone against the door of the tomb, and departed." Matt 27:57-60

There are more than one billion people of a certain religion that have been taught that Jesus never died on the cross. If you are one of those, I would like to unequivocally make it clear to you, that you were told a lie. The truth is in the Bible. Jesus Christ died on the cross openly, with so many witnesses looking. This is a pivotal doctrine that can't be compromised, for without atonement, there is no remission of sin.

Jesus Christ is the lamb of God that was slain before the foundation of the world, according to the scriptures, for the redemption of man. Jesus' blood was shed at Calvary for the remission of our sins. Any faith that promises you paradise or heaven without embracing the death and resurrection of the Lord Jesus Christ, run away from it, for it has nothing to offer you. It is not worth investing your life in it. You need something which works, not fables.

Jesus said He had 'power' to lay down His body and 'power' to raise it up. The Pharisees had heard Him say that when He was teaching. The multitudes were keenly hearing His sayings, that is why, "On the next day, which followed the Day of Preparation, the chief priests and Pharisees gathered together to Pilate saying, "Sir, we remember, while He was still alive, how that deceiver said, 'After three days I will rise.' "Therefore, command that the tomb be made secure until the third day, lest His disciples come by night and steal Him away and say to the people, 'He has risen from the dead. So the last deception will be worse than the first." Matt 27:62-64

Truly you who God has blessed to read this book, 'The Most Powerful People on Earth Revealed,' after hearing the complaints of those Pharisees concerning the resurrection, it does naturally make you wonder why this was very important to them. These people had seen so many of their own taken away by death. No wonder they did not only want to disprove Jesus' claims, but they thought it was just a joke, which was worthy dispelling. The only remedy in this situation, was to watch closely and see what happens after three days. That is what settles that case. Whether the person who died shows up alive and well, able to walk on his feet, able to talk and hear, as well as possibly to do other acts beyond the natural. The Pharisees thought about the entire situation concerning the resurrection of our Lord Jesus Christ, with dread, for they knew that if His words come to pass, then He would truly be the Lord over death.

Amazingly, those people were obsessed with preventing the resurrection of Jesus Christ, other than finding out if what He had claimed to be was true, 'The Son of the Living God.' One who conquered death and has power to raise Himself from the dead.

Guards were put at the tomb of Jesus Christ. Pilate allowed them to have their own guards to secure the tomb. Good enough, the guards became the first witnesses of the Resurrection. 'For the stone was rolled away by an angelic being, "And behold, there was a great earthquake; for an angel of the Lord descended from heaven, and came and rolled back the stone from the door, and sat on it. His countenance was like lightening, and his clothing as white as snow. And the guards shook for fear of him, and became like dead men." Matt 28:2-4

Precious one, Jesus Christ rose from the dead. He conquered death and he defeated it for us His followers.

Jesus Christ, 'Yesu' in Luganda

Even on the day of His death, graves were opened, "And Jesus cried out again with a loud voice, and yielding up His spirit. Then behold the veil of the temple was torn in two from up to the bottom, and the earth quaked, and the rocks were split." Matt 27:50-51

That is very powerful. Not any other man ever lived on earth that we have records of, causing the earth to quake at his or her death. No wonder, Jesus Christ is the most 'powerful' individual to ever grace the world.

The next event is astounding, "and the graves were opened; and many bodies of the Saints who had fallen asleep were raised; and coming out of the graves after His resurrection, they went into the Holy City and appeared to many. So when the Centurion and those with him who were guarding Jesus, saw the earthquake and the things that had happened, they feared greatly, saying, "Truly this was the Son of God." Matt 27:52-54

In the beginnings of this book, God had me to unfold two major topics; 'power' and 'powerful' as a forerunner to the unveiling of the most powerful people on earth. Just looking at those scriptures, you encounter 'power, and 'powerful,' in progress. The power that caused the whole earth to quake, was so glorious that the dead rose from death due to the process of the death and resurrection of Jesus Christ. I completely agree with the Centurion that Jesus is the Son of God.

The Most Powerful People on Earth Revealed

Jesus is alive today. Alive in the believers' hearts. Alive in the Heavenly realm. Alive in our nations, and communities, as well as our neighborhoods. You may not see Him with your natural eyes, but He is right there knocking on the door of your heart. "Behold, I stand at the door and knock. If anyone hears my voice and opens the door, I will come in to him and dine with him, and he with Me." Rev 3:20

I am a Spirit filled believer, I believe in the Lord Jesus Christ. I received Jesus Christ as my personal savior and Lord while a student at Makerere University, Uganda, Africa in Lumumba Hall.

I also went ahead and received the Baptism of the Holy Spirit, with evidence of speaking in tongues, at the New Covenant Church, in Kowloon, Hong Kong, China. While studying Irrigation and Water Conservation Engineering at Hahai University in Nanjing, China. I have been preaching this gospel, that good news, of the death and resurrection of our Lord Jesus Christ, and I have witnessed many from all walks of life, religions, receive Him as their personal Lord and Savior, and their lives have been changed for better, forever.

These people have brought awesome changes in their communities, families, schools, universities, governments, military, police force, hospitals, courts, churches, etc. Truly Jesus is the most powerful person who ever lived on earth. I encourage you to receive Him as your personal savior, as well and this is how you do it: "that if you confess with your mouth the Lord Jesus and believe in your heart, that God has raised Him from the dead, you will be saved. For with the heart one believes unto righteousness, and with the mouth confession is made unto salvation. For the scripture say, 'Whoever believes on Him will not be put to shame." Rom 10:9-11.

In case you have done that, you are now a 'Born Again' Christian. In Luganda language, spoken by people in Uganda, you are a 'mulokole.' And part of the 'Abalokole': That is, you are part of the 'Born Again' Christians-the 'Believers'.

EL-OLAM

EVER-

LASTING

GOD

THE 'BELIEVERS' 'BORN AGAIN' CHRISTIANS 'ABALOKOLE' IN LUGANDA LANGUAGE 'WAUMINI' SWAHILI LANGUAGE

"But as many as received Him, to them He gave the right to become children of God, to those who believed in His name. Who were born not of blood, nor of the will of flesh, nor of the will of man, but of God." John 1:12-13

They Have Power Over Demons

One of the challenges that man and women have faced on the earth, is the nasty spirits referred to as demons; devils; unclean spirits and Satan. We are all aware that when God created man in His image, He meant well for man. He made him in His likeness. "Then God said. "Let Us make man in our image according to Our likeness. Let them have dominion over fish of the sea, over the birds of the air, and over the cattle, over all the earth and over every creeping thing that creeps on the earth." So God created man in the image of God. He created him; male and female: He created them." Gen 1:26-27

Man and Woman were placed in a well prepared, designed environment, the Garden of Eden. It was part of their sustenance and provision. They had to attend to it, from the narrative of the scriptures in Genesis Chapter Two in the Holy Bible, the place was well conditioned to their well-being. They seem to have been healthy, and truly having dominion over the creation.

Adam seemed to have had an extraordinary sound mind. He named the creatures, 'Out of the ground the LORD God formed every beast of the field and every bird of the air, and brought them to Adam to see what he would call them. And whatever Adam called each living creature, that was its name.' Gen. 2:19

Just examining this scripture, you notice that the animals, birds, insects, reptiles, fish, etc., were not hostile to man; it looks like they were friendly and in good company of him. We don't have any record then that the creatures would attack human beings. There was something divine on man that would not allow those animals to devour them.

Man Loses Dominion

Something horrible happened in that garden. A creature referred to as a 'serpent' spoke to the woman, "Now the serpent was more cunning than any beast of the field, which the LORD God had made. And He said to the woman, "Has God indeed said, 'You shall not eat of every tree of the garden'?" Gen 3:1 Now, precious one reading this book, you and I we are in for revelation knowledge. We want to know, whose influence was this serpent under, and what was making this creature talk.

We want to know why is this creature talking to the woman, what is the motive? Why is it interested to know what God spoke to man, whom He made in His image and gave him dominion over every thing created on earth. Was this conversation in good faith or it was out of bad faith. Well, stay with me on this amazing journey of revelation knowledge.

Satan Falls from Heaven

Jesus said in the book of Luke Chapter Ten verse eighteen, "And He said to them, "I saw Satan fall like lightening from heaven." Luke 10:18 Jesus Christ being a Son of God, and Him being in His Father, was there at the beginning of the ages. The existence of our Lord Jesus Christ did not begin on the day He was conceived in Mary's womb; No, No, No. He was, before time. In that passage, He gives us a glimpse of the mystery of the serpent, that appeared to the woman in the garden, at the beginning of creation.

The Bible continues to shed some light on what happened in the heavenly realm, that resulted into the being called Satan – the Old Serpent. "And war broke out in heaven: Michael and his angels fought with the dragon; and the dragon and his angels fought, but they did not prevail, nor was a place found for them in heaven any longer." Rev 12:7-9

In the above scripture, it is very clear that Satan and one-third of the angels transgressed, and because of their disobedience, they lost their place of abode. God had desired them to enjoy goodness, to put it in plain words, these spirits became losers. The original glory that was upon them and in which they were supposed to function, lifted off of them. They turned into evil spirits – fallen angels.

Satan and the other fallen angels envied man, for God had created him in His image and put him on the

Earth, to tend to it and also to be in charge. To this earth Satan fell like lightening; the old serpent, "So the great dragon was cast out, that serpent of old: called the Devil, and Satan, who deceives the whole world, he was cast to the earth, and his angels were cast out with him." Rev 12:9 That is the thing that tempted man and woman with an evil intention of causing them to lose dominion God had given them.

That is the force behind all wickedness you see on the earth; wars, conflicts, injustices, revolutions, uprisings, extremisms, witchcraft, sorcery, hate and all manner of wickedness. The actors on the earth, are not only human beings, but these fallen angels are part of the scene. Beloved, it is very apparent that evil is functional in the world. Any reasonable person knows that something is wrong.

The good news is this: that there are people today, existing on the earth, bestowed on them, the 'power' to arrest these evil spirits: the 'Born Again' Christians. God gave them this divine power. They are the only ones who can bind those spirits by the Word of God. Jesus Christ said to them in the Gospel of Matthew, "Assuredly, I say to you, whatever you bind on earth will be bound in heaven and whatever you loose on earth will be loosed in heaven." Matt 18:18

The Most Powerful People on Earth Revealed

You have to have divine 'power' to stop those destructive, filthy, and killer spirits in their tracks. Those devils can't be fired at by a gun, nor destroyed by a bomb, for they are not flesh and blood, they are not made of natural elements, you can't even lock them up in jail. You don't just shut a natural door on them, for their body composition is spirit. They are invisible to the natural eyes, to say the least, these are talking, moving, cunning disasters. They lost, and their objective is to make everyone else a loser.

They Have No Heaven to Offer

These devils have no heaven to offer to anyone, nor real life to provide, all what they claim on earth, having possession of, they just stole and obtained it through deception.

In the Holy Bible, there is a place in the Gospel of St. Matthew, Chapter Four, talking about the temptation of Jesus Christ by the Devil. "Again the Devil took Him up on an exceedingly high mountain, and showed Him all the kingdoms, of the world and their glory. And he said to Him, "All these things, I will give you if you will fall down and worship me." Matt 4:8-9

In the book of Luke, some extra information is added concerning this narrative of Satan in regard to dominion on earth. "Then the Devil, taking Him up on a high mountain, showed Him all the kingdoms of the world in a moment of time. And the Devil said to Him, "All this authority I will give You, and their glory; for this has been delivered to me, and I give it to whomsoever I wish. "Therefore, if you will worship before me, all will be yours." Luke 4:5-7

Man Delivered those Things to the Devil in the Garden of Eden

In the Garden of Eden, this same devil that tempted Jesus Christ who never budged, tempted the woman and she took of the fruit they were strictly commanded by God not to eat, "And the LORD God commanded the man saying, "Of every tree of the garden you may freely eat, but of the tree of the Knowledge of Good and Evil, you shall not eat, for the day that you shall eat of it, you shall surely die." Gen 2:16-17

Man and woman transgressed the commandment of God, and partook of the fruit of that tree and lost their dominion to Satan. They subjected themselves to the lies and evil control of the fallen angels. That is how the enemy of man's soul gained possession of those things; kingdoms, nations and the goods of the world.

Jesus Christ, the most powerful man who ever lived on earth, rejected the offer of the devil, "And Jesus answered and said to him, "Get behind me Satan! For it is written, "You shall worship the LORD your God, and Him only you shall serve." Luke 4:8 What a great contrast, Jesus knew that in actuality the Devil really has nothing good in it, and all its claim of possession and ownership to what it had stolen craftily mounted to nothing. The truth is, these demons are just thieves, "The thief does not come except to steal, and to kill and to destroy. I have come that they may have life, and that they may have it more abundantly." John 10:10

For you to regain Dominion, you have to have 'power' over those demons. Those evil spirits are real, they can control humans and worst of all, they can enter their bodies and cause very grievous outcomes. In the book of Mark Chapter Five, we run into this kind of a situation. A man's life is stolen away from him by unclean spirits. "And when he had come out of the boat, there met Him out of the tombs a man with an unclean spirit. Who had his dwellings among the tombs, and no one could bind him, not even with chains, because he had often been bound with shackles and chains. And the chains had been pulled apart by him, and the shackles broken in pieces; neither could anyone tame him. And always night and day, he went in the mountains and in the tombs, crying out and cutting himself with stones." Mark 5:1-5

The 'Believers': The 'Born Again' Christians

This man was suicidal; the evil spirits were inflicting wounds on him. Looking at this situation altogether, in the natural, you would think he was self-destructive, but the truth is it was the demons doing that to him.

Isis and gun violence and all acts of hate and murder, demons are very much the reason behind all of that.

For a human being to reach out and take another life because of the difference in their perception of God, is a very pitiful scenario. God is not like that. He is love, and His love is redemptive. He does not want anyone to perish. "For this is good and acceptable in the sight of God our Savior. Who desires all men to be saved and to come to the knowledge of the truth. For there is one mediator between God and man, the man Christ Jesus." 1Tim 2:3-5

The advancing of a religious belief, by killing those who differ with your faith, is demonic, and that persuasion is from the pit of hell. To stop this wickedness, it takes more than military power. The devils behind these atrocities have to be bound and arrested. We thank God for our courageous men and women in uniform, who are trying their best to diffuse the conflicts using natural power; but, one has to have divine power from God, in order to undo the works of the devil. The good news is the 'Born Again' people have been given this 'power'; "Behold I give you the authority to trample on serpents and scorpions, and over all the power of the enemy, and nothing shall by any means hurt you." Luke 10:19

Gun Violence

There has been of recent, an outcry against gun violence. Debaters have analyzed this sad situation. Every day, police, politicians, governments and mental institutions are trying their best to find a solution to this epidemic. Lives of young people, as well as adults, have been ended so drastically, through the acts of some individuals; shootings at school, shootings at theatres, shooting at grocery stores and shootings in homes.

Some individuals have guns that can kill hundreds of people in minutes and seconds. A lot of people say that the cause of this is mental health. Others groups point at these high caliber guns in the hands of bad people, as being the problem. Some simply say, take away the guns and gun violence will be gone. What makes this very paradoxical, is the fact that someone can go and obtain a gun legally, by passing all of the background checks, but no one can guarantee that that person will stay in his "right mind" throughout. Thank God that you have this book in your hands. You will continue to have a better understanding on what the problem is. Gun violence did not start today. In my country, Uganda, especially during those regimens of dictatorship, gun violence was rampant. During World War I, and World War II, violent men and women caused a lot of suffering to humanity through the misuse of guns, bombs, chemicals and other weapons of mass destruction. Bombs were dropped on people's heads, infant babies killed, young students killed, and these were people who had nothing to do with their conflicts. Many thought that that kind of carnage had been brought under control, but reality has proven otherwise. Resulting in having people living in fear today.

I am going to talk to you as a man of God, sent with revelation knowledge from God. God told me that this book would make its way to Congress rooms, state houses, board rooms, hospitals, universities, military installations, and every place of influence you can imagine. Governors of nations, judges, presidents, kings, queens, pastors, teachers will look into it and receive counsel on how to handle this magnitude of complication – gun violence. God instructed me to write it for the betterment of humanity and we start with individuals like you, for everybody is somebody.

The problem of gun violence is worse than what most people think. The remedy is beyond the natural efforts, like that man whom nobody could tame in the book of Mark, Chapter Five, he was suicidal and under the control of evil spirits. Thank God for the efforts of the peace lovers; those who meant well for him and tried to put him under shackles in order to save his life, as well as other people that would be around him.

When Jesus arrived on the scene, the truth about that man's problem as well as acts of violence, was revealed. "When he saw Jesus from afar, he ran and worshiped Him. And he cried out with a loud voice and said, "What have I to do with you Jesus, Son of the Most High God! I implore you by God that you do not torment me." For He said, to him, "Come out of the man, unclean spirit." Mark 5:6-8

While everyone was trying to remedy this problem through the natural way, Jesus Christ addressed it spiritually. I want you to imagine, if that man had a high caliber gun, that could kill in minutes, what amount of damage he would have caused to himself and others.

It is very obvious that a semi-automatic rifle or a high caliber gun can do so much damage when under the control of a human being possessed by devils. That person can easily empty the entire magazine on the unsuspecting people, in a few minutes. Anybody who refuses to see this narrative, is blinded to the truth. Let us say that one had to load one bullet at a time in a gun, in order to shoot, and that person is trying to unleash pain and death to a group of people in a place. The possibilities of arresting that situation is more probable than one using an automatic rifle, which are normally used in war zones, instead of in neighborhoods, where people are not expecting war.

Thank God that there are people who have been empowered to tie the strong man. Nations need to work with them, they are really the most powerful people on earth; their wisdom is needed in this matter of gun violence. These people do not operate under fear, but they have a sound mind, "For God has not given us a spirit of fear, but of power and of love and of a sound mind." 2 Tim 1:7

You should not recommend that everybody have a semi-automatic gun in order to stop gun violence; that kind of response most likely is fear motivated. We have to come to the core of this problem by applying sound counsel. "For the fear of the Lord is the beginning of wisdom, And the knowledge of the Holy One is understanding." Prov 9:10

True and sound counsel is available in regard to this matter. Reduce the firing power of the guns that you make available to the public. That will diffuse the risk of somebody being able to unload bullets on a large number of unsuspecting people, and the rescuer will have time to respond.

The killing of our children on school campuses, as well as people in public places, especially when those demonic powers are unloosed and are searching for those on whom to inflict pain, injury and death by using human beings, must be stopped.

The Believers Can Help

The believers: those people endowed with divine power from above by choice, should be celebrated, sought after and welcomed to prayerfully intervene in our society. The good news is; they are in every nation on the earth.

We should look to these people as a blessing from God. Call them for prayer, especially when you notice something suspicious taking place in your life, at your school, in your place of work, and in your neighborhood. For it could be that those devils have creeped in, to cause divisions and violence. Devils do cause discord in families, homes, governments, the military, police, hospitals and on the streets. Even in jails. The 'Believers'; the 'Born Again' Christians, that carry, the burden removing and yoke breaking power referred to as the anointing, have been empowered by Our Lord Jesus Christ, to destroy the works of the demons, as well as to bind those evil spirits. Beloved, you have to have power to stop the activities of evil forces.

Devils Refuse to Obey a Non-Believer

We have a very interesting incident in the Bible, in the Book of Acts, Chapter Nineteen, whereby the Seven Sons of Sceva, a Jewish Chief Priest tried to help a man who was under the influence and control of violent, evil spirits. It is very likely they were trying to bring this man to sanity. Possibly, they recognized the suspicious behavior of him, that lead them to act.

There were seven of them. That is plenty, a good number. "Also, there were seven sons, of a Jewish Chief Priest, who did so. "And the evil spirit answered and said, "Jesus I know, and Paul I know, but who are you?" Acts 19:15 Precious one, this 'knowing' that this evil spirit is invoking, is not about religion and title. It is about authorization – what authority do you have to command us to leave? Where is the power to enable you to do this!?

What these spirits are saying, is that you being seven as well as strong in the natural, does really amount to nothing. It takes more than muscle power to get rid of these spirits, the next verse brings out this point very, very clearly. "Then the man in whom the evil spirit was leaped on them, overpowered them, and prevailed against them, so that they fled out of that house naked and wounded." Acts 19:16

Imagine if that man had a semiautomatic weapon – a gun that could fire 200 bullets in one minute, in his possession. He would possibly have killed them at a glance. In the previous verses, the Bible says about Paul; a 'Born Again' Christian, that is a believer, "God worked unusual miracles by the hands of Paul. So that even handkerchiefs or aprons were brought from his body to the sick, and the diseases left them, and evil spirits went out of them." Acts 19:11-12

It is very possible that the Seven Sons of Sceva had observed that about Paul. That is why in verse thirteen, the Holy Bible states, "Then some of the itinerant Jewish exorcists took it upon themselves to call on the name of the Lord Jesus over those who had evil spirits, saying, "We exorcise you by the Jesus whom Paul preaches." Acts 19:13

But Paul was not just a religious person, he was never able to cast out devils when he operated as a religious Pharisee. In fact, he himself was being abused

The 'Believers': The 'Born Again' Christians

and bothered by Satan so much, that he used to persecute the Christ-like people, the Believers. However, he became converted drastically, on his way to Damascus, he had letters from the high priest authorizing him to go and perform acts of violence against the people of God, but God being gracious, touched his life and he became one of the 'Born Again' Christians.

That turned him into a believer, and he became part of the most powerful people on earth, the 'Believers.' 'Abakiliza' in Luganda; that is 'Abalokole' (A Ugandan Language). For these people were authorized by Jesus Christ to cast out demons, in His name. "And these signs will follow those who believe: In my name, they will cast out demons, they will speak with new tongues." Mark 16:17

Authorization

I am going to take some time and analyze this word so that we get a better understanding. In the Holy Bible, in the book of John, Jesus said to Pilate during His trial in response to his many questions, "Then Pilate said to Him, "Are you not speaking to me? Do you not know that I have power to crucify you, and power to release you? Jesus answered. "You could have no power at all against me; unless it had been given you from above.

The Most Powerful People on Earth Revealed

Therefore, the one who delivered Me to you has the greater sin." John 19:10-11 This was a very critical time to humanity. The redemption of the human race was on balance; our hope, and redemption lay on the shoulders of Jesus Christ. Jesus was the only one who had the authorization from God the Father to be an atonement for human sins: only His blood was pure enough to do that. He was the Lamb of God, without blemish, slain before the foundation of the world for our sins.

John the Baptist's testimony is this: "The next day John saw Jesus coming towards him and said, "Behold! The Lamb of God, who take away the Sin of the world! "This is He of whom I said. After me comes a man who is preferred before me. For He was before me." John 1:29-30

The way things work out in the universe has a lot to do with authorization. Even to become a Believer – Most Powerful People on Earth; you have to be willing to receive the free gift of salvation, "For God so loved the world that He gave, His only begotten Son, that whoever believes in Him should not perish but have everlasting life." John 3:16

When you believe in Jesus Christ – not religion! And you receive Him in your life as your Lord and Savior,

The 'Believers': The 'Born Again' Christians

You become a 'Believer'. "But what does it say? "Then the Word is near you. In your mouth and in your heart." (that is the Word of faith which we preach): that if you confess with your mouth the Lord Jesus and believe in your heart that God has raised Him from the dead, you will be saved. For with the heart one believes unto righteousness and with the mouth confession is made unto salvation. For the scripture says, "Whoever believes on Him will not be put to shame." Rom 10:8-11

The reason why the seven sons of Sceva, a Jewish high priest, were put to shame when they tried to cast demons out of the man in the Name of Jesus Christ whom Paul preached; was because they had never accepted Jesus Christ as their personal Savior. They only knew about Him. They were not 'Born Again' Christians; 'Abalokole' or 'Muloko' in the Uganda language. These sons of Sceva were just religious people; they did not have the authorization from God to have power over evil spirits.

Getting Help from the Most Powerful People on Earth

We need these peoples' help in every community, neighborhoods, cities, nations and every continent on

The Most Powerful People on Earth Revealed

Earth. I know some of you reading this powerful book, that the Lord lead me to write, have a lot of influence on earth. I strongly advise you to let the believer, preach the Gospel of our Lord Jesus Christ, to the people. There should be prayer in schools, hospitals, as well as at governmental events. Paganism is dangerous, it leaves people exposed to the attacks and control of the demonic.

Most places where the Gospel of our Lord Jesus Christ has been rejected, we see dictatorship, fascism, confusion and chaos.

I lived in China for quite a good number of years, I also lived in Africa for many years. Now, I am living in the United States of America. I can tell the big difference in places where people have freedom of worship; and where the 'Born Again', that is Christ-like believers are actively involved in the day-to-day running of those nations. The atmosphere in those territories is healthier, than in places where there is contempt towards the teachings of our Lord Jesus Christ.

One of the biggest desires of the believers is to share the good news they have with others, and because of that, they tend to engage their communities positively, for you can't win over somebody to God through hate, but with Godly love. Because of that, the people around them tend to feel that somebody believes they are worth something. Everybody wants to be celebrated by somebody. The believers always tell the people that they are so important to God, that is why He gave His only son, Jesus Christ, to die for you on the cross.

The Gospel is not about isolating people from others, but reaching out to others and welcoming them into the community of believers.

The First Time I Met those People – The 'Born Again'

I was a student at St. Henry's College, Kitovu, Africa. A college that prepares young people for greater horizons. It was on a magnificent hill, overlooking the City of Masaka, in the nation of Uganda. It was a boarding school. We lived on campus, and it was for boys only. The founders were Catholic Missionary Brothers. I was in my fourth year at that time, and we were getting ready to sit for exams, that would give us access to the advanced level, once we pass them. The level which I was in at that time, is referred to as the ordinary level: the ordinary level in Uganda includes four years of study, the advanced level is two years of study.

In my class, we took thirteen subjects: English, Math, Economics, Literature, History, Geography, Religious Studies, Chemistry, Accounting, Biology, Physics, Technical Drawing, and Agriculture. We were working so hard on our grades, for we were highly motivated by the teaching staff for excellency.

Everything that we did, we did it to our best, for we had been told that when you have knowledge, you have power to accomplish anything in life. Personally, I scored very high in the day to day tasks at that school. Even though it was during very hard times, for that was the year that the war that removed the dictatorship regime of Idi Amin took place. It was our final year of the Ordinary Level, with war raging all around us. War planes flying over our heads, artillery sounds in our ears, jeeps rushing to the front line, our future was uncertain.

I Meet these People

I was of the Catholic Religion, and I had been a very active person in the Catholic Church since I was nine years old, I used to be an Altar Boy. I would serve in all the Evening Masses throughout the week. So, I had the opportunity to see how those services went. I had a fear for God; and believed that He was there and was a Triune God; God the Father; God the Son; and God the Holy Spirit. I also had heard a lot of readings about the great works that were done by the disciples.

Great works that were done by the Apostles and other believers in Jesus Christ, at that time, testimonies of when they prayed for people, and they were healed, how they could cast out demons, as well as speak in other tongues as the Spirit of God gave them utterance, according to Mark, Chapter Sixteen, verse seventeen, "And He said to them, 'Go into all the world and preach the gospel to every creature. He who believe and is baptized will be saved, but he who does not believe will be condemned. And these signs will follow those who believe: in my name, they will cast out demons, they will speak with new tongues. They will take up serpents and if they drink anything deadly, it will by no means hurt them; they will lay hands on the sick and they will recover." Mark 16:15-18

Well, I never saw any of those miracles take place in the Catholic Church that I attended, as well as those I visited. I use to wonder what was the reason for that. No power; no miracles; no wonders; nothing supernatural!?

My aunt, a wife to a brother of my mother happened to be talking about a people; a fellowship of some professing to be 'Born Again' Christians. She said, that somebody had told her about the Bible reading and tongue speaking people. That people are testifying that when they take those who need prayer to them, miracles happen.

I would like to remind you, those days were very crazy times, we were living in a dictatorship, and so many atrocities were being committed by Idi Amin thugs. People were being thrown into prisons on false allegations, especially on suspicion that they were not in favor of the regime. Others were tortured because they were not Moslems.

Armed robbery was everywhere; the situation was very unruly; there was state run terrorism. The government we had tortured civilians, it was a military rule, with no ethics at all. The bad guys had the guns, which sadly, they bought by using the everyday tax payer's money. May be this is the kind of environment the people in Germany experienced during Hitler's time of dictatorship, for then people lived by the sword and died by the sword. There was no justice in the land. Everything was chaotic, those wicked people made it hard for everyone, regardless of their gender, age or religion, especially, they were extremely hard on the Christians- I mean anybody who talked about Christ; indeed, it was a very bad situation.

People were crying out to God for change, so hearing that, there were some people endowed with divine power to bring a positive difference in our nation, was worth exploring.

I spoke to my aunt, and asked her to take me to those people called 'Born Again' Christians. I wanted to see for myself those mighty things I had heard that were wrought through their lives.

One of the first things the dictatorship did when Idi Amin took power forcibly through a coup, in 1971, was to abolish all nondenominational churches, that is evangelical churches. A decree was issued stating that those gatherings were unlawful, and that the only three groups that they were going to work with was the Catholic Church, Anglican Church and the Islam Faith. Though as time went on, they became hostile to the

Catholics and Anglicans as well, they killed a number of their priests, as well as followers, and declared Uganda to be an Islamic nation. That was between 1971 and 1972. Idi Amin was a Moslem, he and his friends were trying to impose Islam on Uganda, but God said "No!" It never worked. That is the hostile atmosphere in which those believers were functioning in.

The decree that was passed required that anybody found conducting a Christian Evangelistic fellowship, anywhere; whether in the house, hotel, church building, in the open, at school, as long as they are not part of the three religious groups, they had to be arrested, be tortured, as well as thrown into jail, without due process.

This regime was very afraid of those people called, 'Believers'; they were afraid of their prayers, and they viewed them as the worst enemy to their evil acts. Many missionaries, especially those from the U.S.A., were asked to leave immediately. I was young then. I did not understand then, why they were at such enmity against with the Christ-like people. Thanks to God, I know now. These people, the 'Born Again,' could never support wickedness, for they were God fearing people, and truly they had the keys to bring about a turn around – a change of the regime. No wonder Idi Amin, a self-proclaimed life president of Uganda, dreaded them.

I arrive at their fellowship

I came to their fellowship in the evening, and that was between 1979 and 1998. The meeting was in the house, in a town called, Nankulabye, one of the Kampala suburbs. Of course, I was watching my back, for this kind of gathering had been abolished by the government. Something else that I was told about those people, is that they praise and worship God, loudly. They made joyful noise to their God, they could also dance, as well as give testimonies about their relationship with their Savior Jesus Christ.

They also loved telling anybody about Jesus Christ. Whether you are a Moslem, Catholic, Anglican, Jehovah Witness or an atheist, they would just go ahead and witness to you. That made the leaders of those religions get very upset with them. Amazing enough, some of the leaders of those religious groups, had supported Idi Amin's decree to abolish the 'Born Again' believers, for they were upset that many were leaving their religions and becoming 'Born Again' Christians. People were searching for the truth. They were saying, if God is alive, where is He to help us, and where is His delivering power; people were tired of being oppressed, and I was among those who were fed up.

When I went inside the house, I found them praising and singing loudly, making a joyful noise to the Lord God. The whole house was full of jubilant citizens of Uganda, whose rights to freedom of worship had been suppressed by a bad regime. Though they had to pay taxes to the same dictatorship like everybody else. There were two pastors among them, very well dressed in suits. Those men looked smart and clean. They were full of the love of God; you could see it in their eyes. They had Bibles in their hands, and seemed to have peace, joy, love, kindness, gentleness, self-control, etc.

"But the fruit of the Spirit is love, joy, peace, long suffering, kindness, goodness, faithfulness, gentleness, self-control, against such there is no law. And those who are Christ's have crucified the flesh with its passions and desires." Gal 15:22-23 There was harmony and brotherhood in that place. It seemed they esteemed one another highly. For me, that was a miracle and a wonder, by itself.

The 'Believers': The 'Born Again' Christians

Testimonies

Several people whose loved one had been beaten and thrown in jail, rose up to give testimonies of what happened when those pastors prayed for their relatives:-

A Husband is Released from Makindye Military Police Barracks Prison Cell due to Prayers to God in the Name of Jesus Christ

A woman stood up and waved to all to be quiet and attentive, full of joy with tears running down her cheeks. Her husband was picked up from his place of work by the dictatorship's special secret military agents. They claimed that he supported the Tanzanian Forces who were fighting the Idi Amin regime,

This book is not about judging people, nor condemning anybody, but in making the point I have to make, I have to engage history. That helps you to get a better understanding of the pains and suffering of the people. There are many horrific incidences we see on television daily, and we have concerns and feelings for those people who are suffering. But, it is one thing to see it on T.V. and another thing to be sitting right in it. I was right in the midst of that dictatorship of Idi Amin.

I believe that the closest to that regime; were the Hitler Nazi regime in Europe, that caused a lot of death to many families; the Saddam Hussein Regime in Iraq, that gassed its own people with chemical weapons; the confused Apartheid Regime in South Africa, that degraded its own people; slavery in America and Britain that exploited its victims and giving them payments of next to nothing, for their hard work. The Syrian Regime that has caused death to infants, children and adults as well as displacing so many people from their homes, causing them to become refugees in other countries; the evil genocide regime in Rwanda that murdered God's people causing a world-wide outcry, that is the comparison to what Idi Amin's Regime was.

The Idi Amin dictatorship, was a dark moment on earth, in the history of man: It was full of extremism, that was supported by the military men and women whom Idi Amin had gathered around himself – It was a killing machine.

Let Us Continue with the Testimony of the Lady: Her husband was thrown in the trunk of a vehicle.

Her husband was grabbed and dragged out of the government office he worked in, in broad day light. Then, violently thrust in the trunk of the undercover secret intelligence officer's vehicle, with all those on the streets watching. Four armed men with automatic pistols, wielding them in every direction, entered the vehicle and speeded away to an unknown destination, as always, their custom was. During that time, most of the people who were picked up like that, were never seen again, they disappeared forever.

Someone had called the wife of the man, and informed her of what had happened. They had four children, two boys and two girls. The entire family wept that day until they could cry no more.

The next day, they went to the police station to report the incidence. However, the only thing that the police could do, was to record the crime reported, for they said they don't know those people who took their relative, and that they had nowhere, to begin to investigate the matter.

The lady knew someone in the military police, she went and told him what had happened. Unfortunately, the military man told her that he would not do anything about it, for it would put his life in danger.

She had already started grieving and many gathered at the home of one of her relatives to console her and to figure out what to do. This relative happened to have a friend, who was a 'Born Again' Christian. This person happened to be a neighbor of his. So, he invited her to their gathering to be part of the solution seeking committee.

The Most Powerful People on Earth Revealed

The 'Born Again' Christian Suggests Prayer

Before they went further in seeking a solution to their very, very bad problem, the 'Born Again' Christian, a 'mulokole' in Luganda; insisted that the wife and the children of the one that had been snatched away from them by the murderers, should get up and follow her to the place of the pastors of the believers, at the believers' fellowship, to be prayed for.

She told them that those people will pray to God in the Name of Jesus Christ, and that man will be released within seven days!!!.

It was a week since they took the man from his place of work, and all of those people gathered knew the lawlessness of that time. Anyone who could get someone out of their grip alive, within seven days, they would give up all that they have to get that help.

The Mother and the Children Rushed to the Pastors

Volunteers among them quickly followed the 'Born Again' Christ like sister to the place she fellowshipped at; and someone at the knock at the door happily opened for them. There were many others who were waiting for prayer. An usher was at the door attending to the people, they told him urgently what had happened. He moved quickly and informed the pastor's assistant, who speedily informed one of the pastors who was busy in the room praying for someone.

They pray a prayer of agreement

The pastors came out and asked the 'Born Again' Christians: the believers who were in that place to all join hands and pray a prayer of agreement for divine intervention from God. That, the lady's husband, who was snatched away and thrown into a dungeon, where ever it could be, would be released immediately. "Assuredly, I say to you whatever you bind on earth, will be bound in heaven and whatever you loose on earth, will be loosed in heaven." Again, I say to you, that if two of you agree on earth concerning anything that they ask, it will be done for them by My Father in heaven." Matt 18: 18-19

So they asked for the man's release and said 'Lord, do it right away.' The pastors told that lady that the Lord had revealed to them while they were praying, that her husband is still alive, and that God will bring him to her within seven days.

The Man Released within Seven Days

It happened that those prayers had been offered for her during the week I was visiting. This woman was right there, telling her story. She said, that it was on

The Most Powerful People on Earth Revealed

Thursday when she received an anonymous call from some people, saying; 'Go pick up your husband from the military police barracks, at Makindye entrance, at 10:00 a.m. Only come by yourself, if you drive, or with a taxi cab, and we will let you have him.'

The lady did exactly that, she hired a cab and went to the barracks and they delivered to her a man who had been badly tortured, with bruises all over his body and a swollen face. They told her to be grateful that he was still alive, and just drive away without any questions. She picked up her husband and took him to Nsambya Hospital, Emergency Room. They took care of him medically and he is recovering very well.

This lady was very, very thankful for what the Lord God did for her family. She said, those military men were about to kill her husband, through torture. When they were busy torturing him, one of them suddenly changed his mind and said, 'Let us let him go, for he is not worth anything; he seems to be just ignorant,' and they said to him, 'we are sending you back to your people, tell them we did not do anything to you!"

I heard that testimony and glorified God in my heart. I lived in Uganda and was going to school at St. Henry's College, Kitovu right in Masaka City, where you could hear artillery fire as the dictatorship military battled with the combined forces of exiled Ugandans fighting alongside the Tanzanian Army. The people were fighting the regime and were determined to completely throw out the thugs, and relieve the people of Uganda from the suffering they were experiencing during that time.

There is no way that that man would have returned home alive, if it was not divine intervention, done through the lives 'of the most powerful people on earth' referred to as 'the born again' Christians or believers in the Bible.

I heard so many testimonies that day of various divine healings, deliverances, provision of finances and wisdom being obtained to deal with dire situations. All of this was wrought through the hands of God's people. "Most assuredly, I say to you, he who believes in Me, the works that I do you will do also. And greater works, than this he will do, because I go to my Father, "And whatever you ask in my name, that I will do that the Father may be glorified in the Son," John 14:12-13

Beloved, Peter was a believer

Peter, one of Jesus Christ's disciples, who lived about two thousand years ago, who is also referred to as Saint Peter, in line with the writings of the epistles. The Bible refers to 'Believers'; (Born Again) Christians as

The Most Powerful People on Earth Revealed

Saints. "Paul, an apostle of Jesus Christ, by the will of God. To the Saints who are in Ephesus and faithful in Christ Jesus. Grace to you and peace from God our Father and the Lord Jesus Christ." Eph 1:1-2 Peter was busy witnessing for Christ, telling people that they needed to become born again in order to be part of the Kingdom of God.

Now it happened that some disciples of Jesus Christ implored him to come to them quickly, because one of them had died. "At Joppa there was a certain disciple, named Tabitha, which is translated, Dorcas. This woman was full of good works and charitable deeds, which she did. But it happened in those days that she became sick and died. When they had washed her, they laid her in an upper room. And since Lydda was near Joppa, and the disciples had heard that Peter was there, they sent two men to him, imploring him not to delay in coming to them." Acts 9:36-38

Just reading that scripture, you notice that these disciples had a conviction that any of their own could be raised from the dead. They kind of believed that resurrection power was still available to them in the Name of Jesus Christ.

Those believers summoned Peter in hope that something miraculous was going to be performed in their midst. Beloved, that itself is 'powerful' and that puts them in the category of the most powerful people on earth. Many clubs, associations, political parties, and institutions would not even dare think of that, for they know they are not that powerful.

Peter Raises the Dead

"Then Peter arose and went with them. When he had come, they brought him to the upper room. And all the widows stood by him weeping, showing the tunics and garments which Dorcas had made while she was with them. But Peter put them all out, and knelt down and prayed. And turning to the body he said, "Tabitha, arise." And she opened her eyes, and when she saw Peter she sat up. Then he gave her his hand and lifted her up; and when he had called the Saints and widows, he presented her alive. And it became known throughout all Joppa, and many believed on the Lord." Acts 9:39-42

Precious one reading this book, I really think that you do agree with me, that an ordinary person cannot just speak to a dead person, as Peter did and resurrection happens. One has to have authorization from the most powerful man who ever lived on earth; Jesus Christ, the Son of the living God.

These believers were disciples of Christ, and together received their dead that day through their faith in God – Dorcas lived again.

The Most Powerful People on Earth Revealed

That is why we need to know those people, the 'Believers.' For we need their help. Those disciples, and widows utilized that help effectively, and because of that, others received Jesus Christ as their personal Savior and in effect, more were added to the 'most powerful people on earth.'

The Bible says, whatever is born of God, overcomes the world, the believers are of God, they have the nature of God in them. They can speak with Jesus' authority and when they do so, something very good happens. "You are of God, little children and have overcome them, because He who is in you is greater than he that is in the world." I John 4:4 There is a very divisive rhetoric out there; people have taken on very divisive, conflicting identities that sow discord among people. It takes a person crucified to flesh to resist those kind of temptations and extremism.

For one to maintain a good composure, one must have the power of God in your life, no wonder the Word of God states, "For whatever is born of God overcomes the world. And this is the victory that has overcome the world – our faith." I John 5:4

The People Who Prayed for the Release of Peter from prison – were 'Believers'; 'Abalokole' in Luganda that is 'Born Again'

The 'Believers': The 'Born Again' Christians

In the book of Acts, in the Holy Bible, there is a story about a bad king – Herod. This man and his henchmen, were intimidated due to the presence of the Believers in that regime. You find this story in Acts Chapter 12, this man Herod, was such a murderer that he had one of the disciples of Jesus Christ, a brother to John the Apostle, killed with the edge of the sword.

This man lacked decency and honor for good, for instead of celebrating those believers, he saw to it, to be violent against them. After killing James, he kind of thought he was extremely powerful. So he proceeded further to seize another believer; Peter. He put him in prison with the ultimate purpose of killing him.

He had guards, soldiers and a jail as part of the assets, at his exposure, to carry out wickedness. He really felt important and powerful. I want to let you know that possibly if he had obtained a copy of this book, 'The Most Important People on Earth Revealed,' maybe he would not have touched Peter, a 'Believer' and a 'Born Again' Christian. What follows proves my case.

The Believers Prayed and a Big Miracle took Place

The Bible says in the Book of Acts, Chapter Twelve, Verse Five, "So when he had arrested him, he put him in prison and delivered him to four squads of soldiers to keep him, intending to bring him before the people after Passover. Peter was therefore, kept in prison, but constant prayer was offered to God for him, by the church." Acts 12:4-5

Harold had natural weapons at his disposal to do harm. However, the believers had something much more powerful to their benefit – prayer. What they resorted to, prayer completely disarmed the soldiers that were posted to keep Peter bound. All the shackles and chains that were holding Peter, came off him supernaturally. "And when Herold was about to bring him out that night, Peter was sleeping bound with two chains between two soldiers; and the guards before the door were keeping the prison. Now, behold an Angel of the Lord, stood by him and a light shown in the prison, and he struck Peter on the side, and raised him saying, "Arise quickly!" And his chains fell off his hands." Acts 12:7

This Angel came because of the 'Born-Again' Christians prayers

People who can pray to God, as well as have faith to ask God to intervene in a situation like that, when all odds were against the prisoner, and expect divine intervention, truly they have to be 'the most powerful people on earth.' No wonder the Bible says, "If My

The 'Believers': The 'Born Again' Christians

People who are called by My name will humble themselves, and pray and seek My face, and turn from their wicked ways, then I will hear from heaven, and will forgive their sin and heal their land." 2 Chr 7:14

Important Thing to Note

Those people in Acts Nineteen, who prayed had that unique attribute associated with them. Besides being God's people, they were called by the name of God. Jesus said in John Chapter Seventeen, "I have manifested your name to the men whom you have given Me out of the world. They were yours. You gave them to me, and they have kept your Word." John 17:6

These people had the name of Jesus Christ. They most likely prayed to God the Father in the name of Jesus Christ, and sure enough, God answered their prayers.

We need these people today to pray for the healing of our families, those in authority, neighborhoods, cities, institutions, nations, etc., for there is quite a lot of evil out there. As I am writing this book today, students are marching in massive numbers in various states, in the United States of America, protesting gun violence. They do not want to go to school and end up being killed, by someone under the influence of demonic spirits or drugs, as well as unreasonable hate. Today, March fourteen in the year of our Lord two thousand and eighteen, so much is going on. There is an outcry from our kids for help; that is good, they are demanding a change, but more is needed in regard to that.

The people who are called by God's name need to be asked and encouraged to pray for the nation: for God Almighty has promised to answer their prayers in regard to circumstances like this, and bring healing to the land.

Peter is freed from prison

The Bible says, Peter was led out of the jail by an Angel; that is the Angel of the Lord God. The act of freeing him, was so dramatic, in that, none of the soldiers could intervene to stop God from removing Peter from his captives.

Herod's soldiers and guards were rendered powerless; God still does these kind of operations, there is nothing too hard for God. The Bible states that the gate to the city opened on its own accord; that is, it was caused to open supernaturally due to the 'Believers'

The 'Believers': The 'Born Again' Christians

Prayers, "So he went out and followed him, and did not know that what was done by the angel was real, but thought he was seeing a vision. When they were past the first and second guard posts; they came to the iron gate that leads to the city, which opened to them of its own accord; and they went out and went down one street, and immediately the angel departed from him. And when Peter had come to himself, he said, "Now I know for certain that the Lord has sent His angel, and has delivered me from the hand of Herod and from all the expectation of the Jewish people." Acts 12:9-11

The people who were trying to kill Peter, were Jews, his own people; these people were not Ugandans, Americans, Koreans, Indians, Chinese, Nigerians, Kenyans, Mexicans, British, Australians, Egyptians, etc. The point I want to make here is this: wickedness is wickedness, where ever it is found. Sometimes it hides behind a vail, it could be the shade of the skin or the nationality of a person. What we need to

-215-

learn from this is, the problem is not with peoples' outside appearance or their place of origin, it is sin in the heart of a human being. The solution is Jesus Christ.

I had to quote for you from the Holy Bible, this amazing divine intervention that happened when the 'Most Powerful People on Earth,' the 'Believers' who are also called, the 'Born Again,' Christ like; that is 'Abalokole' in the Luganda Language spoken in Uganda, Africa prayed!!!

Herod Struck by an Angel and he dies

Here we are looking at a fundamental regime change. This man who had blood on his hands; of the people of God, and had tormented the people he was supposed to serve faithfully, committing them to injustice without a due process: the Bible says, the angel of the Lord struck him, and he died.

I would like to let you know, that this man full of wickedness, had also just killed the soldiers and guards that he had assigned to keep Peter bound. Possibly he thought they helped the prisoner to escape. That lets you know, that wickedness has no boundaries, no respect for lives, just using people as pawns. He was not at all for them, it was all about him; King Herod and his acquaintances. Some of you reading this book, might be living in these type of circumstances of a fascist regime, where freedom of worship has been tampered with as well as justice.

You could be living in a place where people are killed without due process, it is a tough environment, I have lived under those kinds of regimes and dictatorships, they are horrible. "But when Herod had searched for him and not found him, he examined the guards and commanded that they should be put to death. And he went down from Judea to Caesarea and stayed there." Acts 12:19

When wars take place, and we see civilians killed, many times we are sympathetic towards them. However, sometimes we forget that the soldiers who are used by these dictators to further their cause, are our brothers, sisters, grandparents, mothers, uncles, aunts, etc. These people are put in harm's way, and many times when the dust settles, you find that they died for nothing. They were misled to believe in a cause that was not true. I saw that in the war that removed Idi Amin. Bodies of fallen soldiers were everywhere on the streets, but the dictator got on the plane and ran away. The same phenomenon happened during the Hitler Dictatorship. Bodies of his Dead soldiers were everywhere, they had believed his divisive, dishonesty rhetoric and at the end of the day, they achieved nothing, except to die dishonorably and end up being a plague to humanity.

Misplaced Heroism

I need to teach a bit; because part of what goes on in my office as a Bishop is to address powers, authorities, rulers, principalities and forces of wickedness in high places. I am anointed and appointed to do this, that is part of my Apostolic call. The word apostle means, A Messenger-The sent one.

Many times heroism is misplaced, those who make things really happen are normally behind the scene. Those are the people who had to die on battle fields in the process of protecting the other comrades in arms. It is so serious that those who are really honest, could tell you if it were not 'so and so' who died stopping the enemy fire, from hitting us, we would all have been dead, and this victory you see would not have happened.

Unfortunately, when wickedness is raging, the true heroes are ignored, and the dictators proclaim themselves to be the heroes, to make it even worse, these rulers brain wash the people by giving them as impression that without them, good life is impossible. Sometimes the prayer warriors are not celebrated, but they can be the real engine that turns the wheels in the right direction. Jesus Christ said, he who wants to be first should be a servant to others. I think we have to get the attitude of servanthood back into our lives.

King Herod in the book of Acts, did not portray a good picture of servanthood. No wonder, he faced judgment from God Almighty. There was no truth in him, and his acts were, devil-like. *"You are of your father the devil, and the desires of your father you want to do. He was a murderer from the beginning, and does not stand in the truth, because there is no truth in him. When he speaks a lie, he speaks from his own resources, for he is a liar and the father of it." John 8:44*

Well, this man was struck by the Angel of the Lord and was eaten by worms, and died. "Then immediately, an Angel of the Lord struck him, because he did not give glory to God. And he was eaten by worms and died." Acts 12:23

Do Not Let Yourself Be Struck

The Lord God told me, that this book was going to

end up in the hands of so many people around the world, and some would be changing the course they are taking in order not to be struck by the judgements of God. If you are the kind of a person who is nasty and hostile towards 'believers' in Christ Jesus, the 'Born Again' people, I would like to advise you as a servant of the Most High God, desist from your actions now, for God is greater than man. These people are greater than you, they are 'The Most Powerful People on Earth' and when they cry out to God, God answers their prayers. They are here for a greater cause, the Salvation of man. They even have angels to their service, *"Are they not all ministering spirits sent for to minister for those who will inherit salvation." Heb 1:14* You don't want to be eaten by worms, as what happened to Herod, and he died.

The Good News is: -

The choice to be part of the most powerful people on earth is open to everybody. God is not a respecter of persons. "Then Peter opened his mouth and said: "In truth I perceive that God shows no partiality, "But in every nation whoever fears, Him and works righteousness is accepted by Him." Acts 10:34-35 The door to this kind of power and position is; Jesus Christ

Himself. He says in John, "Jesus said to him, "I am the way, the truth, and the life. No one comes to the Father except through Me." John 4:6 In case you are not yet 'born again' you can become born again right now; you can become a 'Believer' now.

This is how you do it: -

"that if you confess with your mouth the Lord Jesus and believe in your heart that God has raised Him from the dead, you will be saved. For with the heart one believes unto righteousness, and with the mouth confession is made unto salvation. For the Scripture says, "Whoever believes on Him will not be put to shame." Rom 10:9-11

Now that you have done that, you have become part of the most powerful people on earth; 'Abalokole' in Luganda language spoken by most people in Uganda. Find a Holy Bible based teaching church and assemble with the fellow Saints. Always pray to God about everything, for God is with you, and He answers prayers.

They Speak in Tongues – Heavenly Language!

"Likewise the Spirit also helps in our weaknesses. For

we do not know what we should pray for as we ought, but the Spirit Himself makes intercession for us with groanings, which cannot be uttered. Now He who searches the heart, knows what the mind of the Spirit is, because H makes intercession for the Saints according to the will of God." Rom 8:26-27

This is a very amazingly interesting function of supernatural, heavenly help endowed to the believers from God. Most likely, you would agree with me, that prayer is very important and it matters in our everyday activities. Every reasonable person would like to pray a prayer that would be answered by God.

Many people wonder whether they are praying the will of God over their families, cities, towns, neighborhoods and nations, especially in such trying times as these that we are living in.

The good news is, that it is possible for a 'believer,' a 'Born Again' Christian, A 'Mulokole' in Luganda, to tap into the supernatural help of the Holy Spirit, and speak a language or words made available to his or her tongue, supernaturally. These tongues are not learned mentally, such as going to school and being taught a language. For example, I do speak 'Luganda', a language that I learned from my parents, growing up in

The 'Believers': The 'Born Again' Christians

Uganda. I was also taught that language in my primary school. I read a lot of Luganda books, and I am very familiar with that language. I do speak as well as write the English language, they taught me this language at school, in the nation of Uganda. It was part of the syllabus, in college and at primary school.

I speak Chinese as well. It was taught to me at Beijing University of Languages. I satisfied their requirements for graduation, and continued to Hahai University in Nanjing, to study Irrigation and Water Conservation Engineering in Chinese, of course with a Call of God already on my life.

I was a recipient of a full scholarship to study in China. This enabled me to live among the Chinese people. I heard how they spoke their language; I could write it. The Chinese language involves a lot of characters, and it is a very interesting language.

In Uganda at school, they also taught us French. We had to study, listen, read, pronounce words, and debate in an effort to gain control over that language. I am giving you this information to let you know that I know something about languages and what you have to do to learn to speak them. Speaking in a heavenly Language-Tongues, is not learned or acquired the way all other

The Most Powerful People on Earth Revealed

Languages are obtained on earth. No; No; This is a supernatural act by God, empowering human beings to speak as the Holy Spirit gives them utterance, like what took place in the Book of Acts Chapter Two. "And they were all filled with the Holy Spirit and begun to speak with other tongues as the Spirit gave them utterance." Acts 2:4

Utterance: -

It is very interesting to note, that one who speaks in tongues is uttering words made for that particular moment, by the Holy Spirit. When it comes to speaking in tongues in regard to prayer, it is about intercessions for us made by the Holy Spirit, "……., but the Spirit Himself makes intercession for us………." Rom 8:26 The words are presented to the, 'Born Again' Believer supernaturally by divine providence.

These words are not something stored in the brain of a human being, but they come out of the spiritual realm; it is the Holy Spirit of God who effectively empowers the 'Believers' to speak mysteries, "Pursue love, and desire spiritual gifts, but especially that you may prophesy. For he who speaks in a tongue does not speak to men but to God, for no one understands him; however, in the spirit he speaks mysteries." 1Cor 14:1-2, notice this; this person can speak in the spirit!!!

The 'Believers': The 'Born Again' Christians

The Word of God, further states that, this speaking in tongues is very applicable in prayer, "For if I pray in a tongue, my spirit prays, but my understanding is unfruitful. What is the conclusion then? I will pray with the spirit, and I will also pray with the understanding. I will sing with the spirit, and I will also sing with understanding." I Cor 14:14-15

I am a 'Believer'; in Lunganda a 'Mulokole' that is a 'Born Again' Christian, I do speak in tongues. I received the Baptism of the Holy Spirit in the nineties at the New Covenant Bible Believers Church, in Kowloon, Hong Kong, China, while a student of Irrigation and Water Conservation Engineering at Hahai University, Nanjing, China. I do happily confess that this is one of the greatest things that has ever happened to me apart from Salvation when I became born again.

I do pray in the Holy Spirit, and I have met so many fellow 'Believers' around the world who went ahead and received the Baptism of the Holy Spirit with evidence of speaking in other tongues. These people tend to be very effective prayer warriors as well as being very strong in their faith, for he/she who prays in the Spirit edifies himself. "He who speaks in a tongue edifies himself, but he who prophesies edifies the church." I Cor 14:4 Every time we pray in tongues, we believers get strengthened Divinely. We become empowered to carry out exploits. I am talking about those 'Born Again' Christians, who have embraced this grace. "Those who do wickedly against the Covenant he shall corrupt with flattery; but the people who know their God shall be strong, and carry out great exploits." Dan 11:32

We pray in tongues, during the elections in Africa and the tide goes in our favor

We had just had hell on earth; living through the none tolerant of freedom of worship regime in Uganda. A dictatorship regime of Idi Amin, a ruler ship, where many who confessed Jesus Christ as their personal savior, were treated with hostility. Many had been murdered in cold blood, evangelism through preaching the Gospel was banned.

Angry and unruly soldiers were everywhere wielding guns, and breathing death. Many people had fled the nation of Uganda; there was a very big brain drain whereby most people who graduated from colleges, just went out of Uganda to find jobs in peaceable environments.

The 'Believers': The 'Born Again' Christians

Idi Amin had placed his tribal men, as well as people of his religion, the Moslem Faith, in every key position of government. The Army Commanders, Police Commissioners, Government Ministers, Ambassadors, Governors, Mayors, Presidential Advisors, Prison Commissioners, etc. These people were unjustly, everywhere. It was very difficult for a Christian to get a good job in that government.

The Dictatorship had been overthrown through a very fierce war, where many were left dead. The man who had imposed himself on the Ugandan people, and proclaimed himself to be a life president, fled the nation and went to live in Saudi Arabia. Most of his henchmen were killed, and the rest fled to South Sudan and Congo, completely helpless and defeated due to the prayers of the 'Born Again' people all over the world.

Constant prayers were offered to God for people in the country of Uganda, many 'Believers' in various countries around the world prayed in tongues for the peace of Uganda. I really believe, I am one of those who is still alive today, because of those prayers. People in Tanzania prayed, those in Kenya prayed, those in the United States of America prayed, others in China and Hong Kong prayed, and God sent the answer.

The Most Powerful People on Earth Revealed

The answer was – The Tanzanian Army. These people were very disciplined and they had a number of Ugandan soldiers fighting along with them. Even the Chinese were part of the fighters. 'Born Again' people were part of the fighters. These people were not just shooting at everything that moves; but they knew who exactly they were looking for, the thugs – Idi Amin and his henchmen.

God gave them so much help that even though the dictatorship regime had invested most of the taxpayer's money in buying very costly weapons, they were no match to the invading army of the Tanzanians. The Tanzanian fighters referred to one another as 'Ndugu', which is a Swahili word for 'Brotherhood.' They used this brotherhood language even towards the civilians in Uganda. We felt a relief from madness: really God sent those people to help.

Are you surprised that when 'the Most Powerful People on Earth' prayed, the soldiers of the Idi Amin regime were rendered powerless?

After that regime, another group of rulers followed, but they could not get their acts together, but in the process, the church started regaining its position of authority in Uganda.

The 'Believers': The 'Born Again' Christians

The 'Born Again' people started witnessing and preaching the Gospel of our Lord Jesus Christ, little by little, amidst a number of hostile ones; those who did not want freedom of worship in our nation.

They wanted to control the government again through the narrow denominational belief, and uninformed thinking, that would end up subjecting everybody to their religions. That was very much reflected in the campaigns that took place between 1994 and 1996 whereby some political parties were not ready for freedom and justice.

We Pray in Tongues

I happened to be pastoring a church in Kampala during that time. It was on the Eastern side of the capital city and we were very busy evangelizing; telling people that God is love and He sent His son to die for them. We loved the people of God, and we were doing all we knew to help them. "He who does not love, does not know God, for God is love." I John 4:8

There were many 'Believers' churches and fellow ships in various places around the nation. The 'Born Again' Christians were very, very active evangelizing, preaching the Word of God to everybody across their path. Many people heeded the Gospel, and they opened their hearts to the teachings of Jesus Christ, the message of peace. The nation started turning around for the better. We started having peace and prosperity.

We, the believers, especially the pastors, made a decision to change the tide of the elections through prayer and educating people about the importance of justice and freedom of worship. We gave people the opportunity to know the candidates, and what they stood for, so that they may make a good judgment on which party should be in office.

Above all, we prayed to God in tongues. "Confess your trespasses to one another, and pray for one another that you may be healed. The effective fervent prayer of a righteous man avails much." Jam 5:16 That is exactly what we did. A good number of pastors came together and prayed in tongues for the nation. Here are a few of the participants: Dr. Kiganda; Dr. Joseph Serwadda; Dr. Daniel Nkata; Dr. Mugerwa; Professor Simion Kayiwa; Dr. Robert Kayanja; Dr. Abed Bwanika; Bishop Leonard Kayiwa; Dr. Jackson Ssenyongo; Bishop Grivas Mussissi; Pastor Tina; Dr. Lumara; Dr. Patrick Osile, Prophetess Patricia Baradi and many others.

We communicated to our congregations nation-wide, the need to pray and vote right. We also asked our brothers and sisters in Christ, the 'Born Again'

The 'Believers': The 'Born Again' Christians

Christians, 'Aboluganda mu Yesu: Abalokole' in the Luganda Language, worldwide to pray with us and for us in the heavenly language – tongues.

God graced me to preside over a number of those very important gatherings, I chaired and facilitated those 'winners' meetings, with a number of very anointed preachers. Surely, our efforts were rewarded. Uganda ended up with a government that respected freedom of worship. This is what we prayed for, and God Almighty granted it.

We do need the prayers, of the Born Again Believers today, in regard to every thing, for it is them that have humbled themselves and sought the mercies of God and are well equipped by the Holy Spirit of God to pray and destroy demonic activity. "For we do not wrestle against flesh and blood, but against principalities, against powers, against the rulers of the darkness of this age, against spiritual hosts of wickedness in the heavenly places. Therefore take up the whole armor of God, that you may be able to withstand in the evil day, and having done all, to stand." Eph 6:12-13

Beloved of God, no wonder the Bible admonishes us to pray always with all prayer, and supplication in the Spirit. The ability to pray in tongues makes the 'Believers' the 'most powerful people on earth.' For this venue can only function through a yielded to the Holy Spirit, born again Christian. Always remember, most of the time; God will take you, as far as you are willing to go.

The men and women of God who came together at a very critical moment in the Nation of Uganda, to pray, were just willing vessels, for God through them to heal the nation. These men and women of God; who stand in the offices of; apostles, prophets, evangelists, teachers, pastors, they put aside their valuable schedules and willingly stood in the gap for the whole nation. By the way, they have preached the Gospel all over the world and God has confirmed the Word preached through signs and wonders following.

They Live Divinely – with Godly Love

"Now hope does not disappoint, because the love of God has been poured out in our heart by the Holy Spirit. Who was given to us." Rom. 5:5

This is a very important analogy, concerning one of the most important aspect of life – love. Every reasonable person wants to be loved. People want to be celebrated through love, as well as recognized. It is love that holds families together. In the Holy Bible, the writer of the epistles to the believers at Corinth; referred to as the Corinthians; Paul a 'Believer' himself, and an Apostle of Jesus Christ. under the guidance of the Holy Spirit, wrote this to everyone. "Though I speak with the language of men and of angels, but have not love. I have become a sounding brass or a clanging cymbal." 1 Cor 13:1   In this illustration, Paul uses a very interesting format to make an extremely important point.

That it is not necessarily what you say, but how you say it. My wife, Pastor Gail Kayiwa tells that very well. She always tells the people that how you say something matters; you have to say it with love.

Paul in his letter, uses two divine examples; the speaking in tongues of men divinely, while empowered by the Holy Spirit and the speaking in heavenly tongues. This kind, took place in the Book of Acts, Chapter Two, "And when this sound occurred the multitude came together and were confused, because everyone heard them speak in his own language. Then they were all amazed and marveled. Saying, to one another 'Look are not all these who speak Galileans? "And how is it that we hear, each in our own language, in which we were born?' Acts 2:8

This gift or divine empowerment is from God, and the 'Born Again' believers can function in it, in order to bring good news as well as healing to the hurting world. It is part of the greatest gifts from God Almighty. The explanation is that, anything done not in love is lacking substance. Love is a must. It is like having so much money in one's possession, but lacking compassion to share it with those who are hurting.

The truth is, there is no self-made person, all of us are beneficiaries of others' contributions. We thrive on everybody's efforts. God made it that way, He gave different gifts to different people. When these gifts are shared, then the system of humanity works properly.

Saint Paul, a 'Believer,' goes on to refer to the speaking of the tongues of angels; hereby clearly revealing that what he is talking about is divinely inspired: He had to use this example to make a point, even though he spoke in tongues himself. "I thank my God, I speak with tongues more than you all." I Cor 14:18

Paul knew how important these graces are, but in order to make a heart touching point, he had to work with that level of magnitude, in order to let you know that love is extremely important, and we have to have it.

Attributes of Love

"Love suffers long and is kind; Love does not envy, Love does not parade itself, is not puffed up; does not behave rudely, does not seek its own, is not provoked, thinks no evil, does not rejoice in iniquity, but rejoices in the truth; bears all things, believes all things, hopes all things, endures all things. Love never fails............."1 Cor 13: 4-8 I know you are saying in your heart right now; that, Oh, I need to have that love. My husband needs to have it, too, in case you are married; my siblings need this virtue; the people in our neighborhood need it too; the students at our school need it too; etc.

The other unique aspect of this love presented here – the agape love; that is the God kind of love, it never fails. This love is poured into the heart of a believer by the Holy Spirit: it is found in the heart of one who has received Jesus Christ as their personal Savior and Lord.

Martin Luther King, Jr., one of the most effective civil rights activists, was moved by the Agape love.

I really believe this example I am tapping into is a good one. The fact that I am a 'Born Again' Christian, I try my best to choose proper words when communicating what God has placed within my reach.

The messages of Rev. Dr. Martin Luther King, Jr., to the world, were amazing. This man was able to communicate in such a loving way to the haters and those hated; what he said made sense to many and diffused complicated conflicts. He talked about the need of people of all kinds, holding hands together peacefully and marching forward on the journey of life, in hope. Martin Luther King, Jr. had a love language, no wonder he is among the most powerful people who ever lived on earth.

He helped to make the world a better place for everyone one to live in. I really give glory to God that a 'Believer'; a born again preacher, was celebrated by the most powerful nation on earth, the United States of America, when they erected a monument in honor of him, and his love, for people of all kinds.

All reasonable people agree that; that man's message, and the way that it was delivered, spoke to the goodness in humanity: the image of God, in which man was originally created. What I have done in this book, is to reveal to you the source of his love and effectiveness.

I come from East Africa, and I have seen diversity, but it is not comparable to the United States of America. This nation, has all kinds of shades of people, it is like shades united. This is a country where you find people from Africa, Europe, Asia, South America, Australia and North America. America is complex. To get any particular person to be a leader, or a president, of the United States, you have to get votes from all these different people. You can't just win based on one group

The 'Believers'; The 'Born Again' Christians
you need support from others; the presidency of Barack
Obama with his wife, an attorney who graduated from
Princeton and Harvard University, Michelle Obama,
were a mystery to so many people. Many did not think
it could happen, but Martin Luther King, Jr. had already
foreseen it in his prophetic utterances.

These two leaders, Barack Obama and Michelle
Obama, with their Vice President Joe Biden, was a clear
fulfillment of Martin Luther King's revelation in his
great speech, 'I Have a Dream.' The diversity in the
presidency of this man, Barack Obama, a graduate of
Columbia University and Harvard University; whose
father was from East Africa and his mother had an Irish
ancestry, surpassed all prior presidencies. Rev. Martin
Luther King, Jr.'s words echoed everywhere during the
campaigns that gave President Barack Obama and his
wife Michelle Obama a two term presidency, for words
of love matter.

Martin Luther – The Reformer

I would like to introduce you to another interesting
'Believer' a 'Born Again' Christian. This German
Priest through his life, God brought a major reformation
to the benefit of His people. He preached that salvation
is not by works, but through grace by faith. That was
profound: his teachings pointed people to the Bible,
and they found Jesus Christ as their Lord and Savior.
This man sacrificed his life, his possessions to inform

the world the truth about salvation, and many are 'Born Again' today, because of that reformation.

There are other 'Believers' like; Bishop Benson Idahosa from Africa; Oral Roberts from The United States of America; Paul Crouch and His wife Jane Crouch; Deo Balabye Ekubo from Africa; Billy Graham from the United States of America; Andrew Murray from South Africa, Katherine Kulman from the United States of America, the list goes on and on.

These 'Born Again' Christians have shared the Word of God with everybody within their reach. They are part of 'The Most Powerful People on Earth.' Though they are not physically with us anymore, but like Saint Paul, Saint Peter, Saint John, they are alive in the presence of God.

This book is about 'The Most Powerful People on Earth Revealed.' This is a collective revelation of an entity; a people who exist today and have also existed yesterday, and will exist in the future. Some of their names may not be in any book, anywhere, but what matters is the fact that God's love was poured in their hearts, and they used it to make the lives of people better.

The Rapture – The Catching Away of the Believers

The 'Believers': The 'Born Again' Christians

Precious one reading this book, I would like to introduce you to something that will cause your ear to tingle in case you are not yet born again; the Rapture. "But I do not want you to be ignorant, brethren, concerning those who have fallen asleep, lest you sorrow as others who have no hope. For if we believe that Jesus died and rose again, even so God will bring with Him those who sleep in Jesus. For this we say to you by the word of the Lord, that we who are alive and remain until the coming of the Lord will by no means precede those who are asleep. For the Lord Himself will descend from heaven with a shout, with the voice of an archangel, and with the trumpet of God. And the dead in Christ will rise first. Then we who are alive and remain shall be caught up together with them in the clouds to meet the Lord in the air. And thus we shall always be with the Lord. Therefore, comfort one another with these words." I Thess 4:13-18

These people, the 'Born Again' they are a gift to humanity, and they are only still on the earth because of God's desire that none should perish, but at any time, they could be caught up in the air, supernaturally, at the return of the most powerful man who has ever lived on the earth, Jesus Christ. This will happen in God's timing. Just that makes them, 'The Most Powerful People on Earth.'

Let me try to explain to you a little bit more of what

will happen; there will be a shout in the heavens at the trumpet sound of an arch angel, the dead: those who received Jesus Christ as their personal savior before they passed on, will suddenly come out of the graves and shall put on a glorified body and be caught up in the heavens with the Lord Jesus Christ.

Those who remain; that is the 'Born Again' Christians, will be changed in a moment, and they will be caught away into the air to meet their Lord, Jesus Christ. These people will end up with glorified bodies as well. In other words, they will disappear into the sky to meet the Lord.

There is no other teacher or founder of a religious group who offers this promise of being caught up with Him in heaven, at His return, for His Bride except Jesus Christ, the Son of the Living God.

These people will disappear from their place of work, homes, streets, highways, churches, that is from all nations. When this rapture takes place, the whole world will be shaken up and it will never remain the same again, for the departure of those people will usher in the most difficult times ever experienced on earth.

Let's say that there is a married couple, one is a believer and the other is not. At the Rapture, the believer will be taken away into the heavens to meet the Savior and Lord, Jesus Christ. But the nonbeliever will remain here on the earth to go through the Tribulation. People will be at their place of work, taking care of business as usual and suddenly the trumpet will sound, every 'Believer' in that bank, military barracks, beauty parlor, school, hospital, church, library, football arena, state house, steak house, Congress, police, battlefield, restaurant, train, plane, bus, car, etc., will be caught away into the air at the appearance of Jesus Christ! You don't want to miss this.

Families will be divinely separated, unless all of them are believers. In case the president of any nation is a born again Christian, that country will either conduct new elections or swear in the vice president, if he happens not to be a believer. I am looking forward to that glorious day! I hope it happens when I am still alive.

For you reading this book, in case you have never given your life to Jesus Christ, to be your Lord and Savior, it is time to do it right now. For this rapture can happen at any time. You don't want to be left behind. Join 'the most powerful people on earth.'

Love in Soul Winning

It is very difficult to win over people to the Salvation of our Lord Jesus Christ, if you are not a lover of God's people. Human beings tend to move towards love, especially the love of God. God knows that; that is why

The Most Powerful People on Earth Revealed

The love of God, according to Romans Chapter Five is poured into the willing vessels; those people who have received Jesus Christ as their personal savior and have become a new creation. "Therefore, if anyone is in Christ, he is a new creation, old things have passed away; behold all things are become new." 2 Cor 5:17

These people, the 'Believers,' can love even when all odds are against them. I remember a Saint from Uganda, a believer in our Lord Jesus Christ, an Evangelist: Bishop Festo Kivengare, who wrote a book with a title, 'I Love Idi Amin', and many were puzzled why he could dare say such a thing about a man who killed so many people, and he even tried to kill Festo Kivengare.

Bishop Festo Kivengare was a fiery gospel preacher from Africa. When you got around him, you could feel God's love, this man loved people. He was really, a 'Born Again' Christian. He was very active in the Anglican Church, Episcopal Church, and outside the church walls. He preached at university campuses, and when he ran away from being killed by Idi Amin in Uganda, he continued spreading the Gospel in the United States and other countries.

Amidst all the atrocities Idi Amin carried out against the people of Uganda, whereby he also killed a man of

The 'Believers': The 'Born Again' Christians

God, Arch Bishop Janani Luwumu, who was serving Uganda, Tanzania, Congo, Rwanda and Burundi, his fellow comrade in the Gospel. Still, Festo Kivengere saw him as a potential convert; one who deserved a chance to repent; that is the love of God.

The dictatorship murdered Janani Luwumu for telling them that they needed to stop killing people and that justice should be for all. Luwumu was a 'Born Again' Christian, who sympathized with the people. There is a road named in his honor in Uganda.

The love of God found in the heart, of Mother Grace Tucker, a woman of God, who lived in the United States of America, Tulsa, Oklahoma was amazing. This woman of God cared for the homeless, fed the hungry, clothed those who needed clothing, provided shelter for needy people, as well as preached the Gospel of Our Lord Jesus Christ, with such a conviction and love, that would cause any body to reevaluate their faith. Dr. Grace Tucker was a born again believer.

William J. Symour, referred to as a father to Pentecostalism, in greater America, was a wonder. This man and other 'Believers' had a strong desire to pray for people all over the world; they desired God's will to be done on earth as it is done in Heaven, Pastor William J. Symour sought the Lord with all his heart and God answered back. He became filled with the Holy Spirit with evidence of speaking in tongues. He obtained a heavenly prayer language which literally empowered him to encourage every 'Believer' to get this grace in their lives so that they may through prayer, bring a change on earth. This caused the Revival of Pentecostalism in the world, where many gladly received the Baptism of the Holy Spirit, with evidence of speaking in other tongues.

Bishop G.E. Patterson, a 'Believer' from the United States of America, who presided over a big body of believers, loved God; praised and danced for the Lord. He was part of the fruits of a man of God: Apostle Charles Harrison Mason, who preached the Gospel under a very strong anointing, and many became part of 'the most powerful people on earth,' the 'Born Again' Christians.

Brother Kenneth E. Hagin, was a very interesting teacher of the Word. He let the brethren know that faith in God still works. This man founded a Bible School in the United States of America, whose graduates have blessed nations. He operated in a very strong prophetic anointing; that anointing changed so many lives, and brought joy to the earth. Of course he did not do all of this by himself, it happened, that, Rev. Hagin, was part of the 'Born Again' Christians.

The 'Believers': The 'Born Again' Christians

Another man, worthy of talking about is, Pastor Frank Lutaya from Uganda, Africa; many very anointed preachers who have preached the Word, around the world, graced his path. He taught them the best that he knew at that time. He loved God, and the people of God. He believed in evangelism, and he is one of those men of God who prayed for the healing of the nation of Uganda. He preached the Gospel in very difficult times; during the dictatorship. He is part of the 'Born Again' Christians.

"See that you do not refuse Him who speaks. For if they did not escape who refused Him who spoke on earth, much more shall we not escape if we turn away from Him who speaks from heaven, whose voice then shook the earth; but now He has promised, saying, "Yet once more I shake not only the earth, but also heaven. Now this, "Yet once more, indicates the removal of those things that are being shaken, as of things that are made. That the things which cannot be shaken may remain. Therefore, since we are receiving a kingdom which cannot be shake, let us have grace, by which we may serve God acceptably with reverence and godly fear. For our God is a consuming fire." Heb12:25-29

The Most Powerful People on Earth Revealed

After you have read this book, I believe now you are in a better position to know if your name is written in the Lamb's Book of Life. Feel free to write your name on this page in this very, very powerful book, written under revelation knowledge, from the Lord God Almighty: in case you are a 'Born Again' Believer.

Put your testimony here

Jehovah-
Shammah

The Lord is

Present

Please be a partner to this ministry by sowing your seed in this good ground, that we may get this message to as many as possible.

Honor the Lord with your possessions and with the first fruits of all your increase; so your barns will be filled with plenty, and your vats will overflow with new wine. Proverbs 3:9-10

**Many have done that and God
Has healed them miraculously**

Leonard Kayiwa Ministries

P.O. Box 1898

Bolingbrook, Illinois 60440

(224)440-6992

kayiwaministries@yahoo.com

THE ISAIAH 58 BLESSING:

You can also receive a copy of this book for a donation of $25.00 or more in support of the drive to help orphans.

Bishop Leonard MP Kayiwa founded a 501©3 tax exempt church organization for helping orphans in different countries in Africa.

This organization is registered in the U.S.A. and in Africa. It is called:

AFRICAN CHILDREN BENEVOLENCE FOUNDATION INTERNATIONAL, INC.

We shall send you a tax-deductible receipt for your gift towards helping God's children – the orphans.

We will also send you a copy of this beautiful book.

Make your check payable to:

A.C.B.F.I., Inc. or African Children Benevolence Foundation International, Inc.

P.O. Box 1898, Bolingbrook, IL 60440

www.acbfii.org; www.ministeringtogod.com

acbfii@yahoo.com   God bless you!!!

"For this is good and acceptable in the sight of God our Savior, who desires all men to be saved and to come to the knowledge of the truth. For there is one God and one Mediator between God and men, the Man Christ Jesus, who gave Himself a ransom for all, to be testified in due time," I Timothy 2:3-6

"But what does it say? "The word is near you, in your mouth and in your heart (that is, the word of faith which we preach): that if you confess with your mouth the Lord Jesus and believe in your heart that God has raised Him from the dead, you will be saved. For with the heart one believes unto righteousness, and with the mouth confession is made unto salvation. For the Scripture says, "Whoever believes on Him will not be put to shame." Romans 10:8-11

Quotations in the English Language

"But as many as received Him, to them He gave the right to become children of God, to those who believe in His name: who were born, not of blood, nor of the will of the flesh, nor of the will of man, but of God." John 1:12-13

Jesus answered and said to him, "most assuredly, I say to you, unless one is born again, he cannot see the kingdom of God." John 3:3

"Ekyo kye kirungi, ekikkirizibwa mu maaso g"Omulokozi waffe Katonda, 4 ayagala abantu bonna okulokoka, era okutuuka mu kutegeerera ddala amazima. 5 Kubanga waliwo Katonda omu, era omutabaganya wa Katonda n"abantu omu, omuntu Kristo Yesu, 6 eyeewaayo abe omutango olwa bonna; okutegeeza kulibaawo mu ntuuko zaakwo:" 1Timoseewo 2:3-6

This is Luganda language (Uganda) Africa

"Naye bwogera butya? Nti, Ekigambo kiri kumpi naawe, mu kamwa ko, ne mu mutima gwo: kye kigambo eky'okukkiriza kye tubuulira: 9 kubanga bw'oyatula Yesu nga ye Mukama n'akamwa ko, n'okkiriza mu mutima gwo nti Katonda yamuzuukiza mu bafu, olirokoka: 10 kubanga omuntu akkiriza na mutima okuweebwa obutuukirivu, era ayatula na kamwa okulokoka." Abaruumi 10:8-10

"Naye bonna abaamusembeza yabawa obuyinza okufuuka abaana ba Katonda, be bakkiriza erinnya lye" Yokkaana 1:12

3 Hili ni zuri, nalo lakubalika mbele za Mungu Mwokozi wetu;

4 ambaye hutaka watu wote waokolewe, na kupata kujua yaliyo kweli.

5 Kwa sababu Mungu ni mmoja, na mpatanishi kati ya Mungu na wanadamu ni mmoja, Mwanadamu Kristo Yesu;

6 ambaye alijitoa mwenyewe kuwa ukombozi kwa ajili ya wote, utakaoshuhudiwa kwa majira yake.   1 Timotheo Mlango 2:3-6

Swahili Language, Africa

8 Lakini yanenaje? Lile neno li karibu nawe, katika kinywa chako, na katika moyo wako; yaani, ni lile neno la   imani   tulihubirilo.
9 Kwa sababu, ukimkiri Yesu kwa kinywa chako ya kuwa ni Bwana, na kuamini moyoni mwako ya kuwa Mungu   alimfufua   katika   wafu,   utaokoka.
10 Kwa maana kwa moyo mtu huamini hata kupata haki, na kwa kinywa hukiri hata kupata wokovu. Warumi Mlango 10: 8-10

12 Bali wote waliompokea aliwapa uwezo wa kufanyika watoto wa Mungu, ndio wale waliaminio jina lake; Yohana Mlango 1: 12

Make
Sure
You
Get
Born
again

please

3   这是好的，在神我们救主面前可蒙悦纳。

4   他愿意万人得救，明白真道。

5 因为只有一位神，在神和人中间，只有一位中保，乃是降世为人的基督耶稣。

6 他舍自己作万人的赎价。到了时候，这事必证明出来。   提

摩太前书 2 章 3-6

8 他到底怎么说呢？他说，这道离你不远，正在你口里，在你心里。就是我们所传信主的道。

9   你若口里认耶稣为主，心里信神叫他从死里复活，就必得救。

10 因为人心里相信，就可以称义。口里承认，就可以得救。   罗

马书 10 章 8-10

12 凡接待他的，就是信他名的人，他就赐他们权柄，作神的儿女。   約

翰福音 1 章 12

Chinese Language

Following, is The Lord's Prayer in 12 languages

of

the world.

14 For as many as are led by the Spirit of God, these are sons of God.

15 For you did not receive the spirit of bondage again to fear, but you received the Spirit of adoption by whom we cry out, "Abba, Father."

16 The Spirit Himself bears witness with our spirit that we are children of God,

17 and if children, then heirs—heirs of God and joint heirs with Christ, if indeed we suffer with Him, that we may also be glorified together.

18 For I consider that the sufferings of this present time are not worthy to be compared with the glory which shall be revealed in us.

19 *For the earnest expectation of the creation eagerly waits for the revealing of the sons of God.*

20 For the creation was subjected to futility, not willingly, but because of Him who subjected it in hope;

21 because the creation itself also will be delivered from the bondage of corruption into the glorious liberty of the children of God.

22 For we know that the whole creation groans and labors with birth pangs together until now.

The Lord's Prayer in English

[8] *"Therefore do not be like them. For your Father knows the things you have need of before you ask Him.* [9] *In this manner, therefore, pray:*
Our Father in heaven,
Hallowed be Your name.
[10] *Your kingdom come.*
Your will be done
On earth as it is in heaven.
[11] *Give us this day our daily bread.*
[12] *And forgive us our debts,*
As we forgive our debtors.
[13] *And do not lead us into temptation,*
But deliver us from the evil one.
For Yours is the kingdom and the power and the glory forever. Amen.[b]

[14] *"For if you forgive men their trespasses, your heavenly Father will also forgive you.* [15] *But if you do not forgive men their trespasses, neither will your Father forgive your trespasses. Matt 6:8-15*

THE LORD'S PRAYER IN CHINESE

8 不可像他们那样，因为在你们祷告以前，你们的父已经知道你们的需要了。

9 **"你们应当这样祷告，**

" '**我**们天上的父，

愿人们都尊崇你的圣名，

10 愿你的国度临，

愿你的旨意在地上成就，就像在天上成就一样。

11 **求你今天**赐给我们日用的饮食。

12 **饶恕我们的罪，**

就像我们饶恕了得罪我们的人。

13 **不要**让我们遇见诱惑，

救我们脱离那恶者。

因为国度、权柄、荣耀都是你的，直到永远。阿们！'

THE LORD'S PRAYER IN SWAHILI

⁸ Msiwe kama wao, kwa sababu Baba yenu anajua mahitaji yenu hata kabla hamjaomba." ⁹ Basi msalipo ombeni hivi: 'Baba yetu uliye mbinguni jina lako litukuzwe. ¹⁰ Ufalme wako uje, mapenzi yako yafanyike hapa duniani kama huko mbinguni. ¹¹ Utupatie leo riziki yetu ya kila siku. ¹² Na utusamehe makosa yetu kama sisi tulivyokwisha kuwa samehe waliotukosea. ¹³ Na usitutie majaribuni, bali utuokoe kutokana na yule mwovu,' [Kwa kuwa Ufalme na nguvu na utukufu ni vyako milele. Amina.] ¹⁴ Kama mkiwasamehe watu makosa yao, Baba yenu wa mbinguni atawasamehe na ninyi; ¹⁵ lakini msipowasamehe watu makosa yao,

THE LORD'S PRAYER IN RUSSIAN

⁸ Не уподобляйтесь им, потому что Отец ваш знает, в чём вы нуждаетесь, прежде чем вы попросили его об этом. ⁹ А потому молитесь вот как:

„Отец наш Небесный,
    да будет свято имя Твоё.
¹⁰ Да наступит Царство Твоё.
    Пусть исполнится воля Твоя на земле,
    как и на Небе.
¹¹ Пошли нам хлеб насущный на каждый день
¹² и прости нам грехи наши,
    как мы простили тех, кто причинил нам зло.
¹³ Не подвергай нас искушению,
    но избавь нас от лукавого"
[Так как Тебе принадлежат и Царство,
    и сила, и Слава вовеки. Аминь.] [a]

¹⁴ Потому что если вы простите людей за их грехи, то и Отец ваш Небесный тоже простит вам. ¹⁵ Если же вы не простите тех, кто причинил вам зло, то и Отец ваш не простит ваши грехи».

[8] 너희는 그들을 본받지 말아라. 너희 아버지께서는 너희가 구하기 전에 너희에게 필요한 것이 무엇인지 다 알고 계신다.

[9] 그러므로 너희는 이렇게 기도하여라. '하늘에 계신 우리 아버지, 아버지의 이름이 거룩히 여김을 받게 하시고

[10] 아버지의 나라가 속히 오게 하소서. 아버지의 뜻이 하늘에서 이루어진 것같이 땅에서도 이루어지게 하소서.

[11] 우리에게 날마다 필요한 양식을 주시고

[12] 우리가 우리에게 죄 지은 사람들을 용서해 준 것처럼 우리 [a]죄를 용서해 주소서.

[13] 우리가 시험에 들지 않게 하시고 우리를 [b]악에서 구해 주소서. [c](나라와 권세와 영광이 영원토록 아버지의 것입니다. 아멘.)'

[14] "너희가 다른 사람의 죄를 용서하면 하늘에 계신 너희 아버지께서도 너희를 용서하실 것이다.

[15] 그러나 너희가 다른 사람의 죄를 용서하지 않으면 너희 아버지께서도 너희 죄를 용서하지 않으실 것이다

THE LORD'S PRAYER IN KOREAN

THE LORD'S PRAYER IN ARABIC

أباكُمْ لِأَنَّ ،مِثلَهُمْ تَكُونُوا لا لِذَلِكَ 8 .كَلامِهِمْ كَثْرَةِ
تَطلُبُوه أنْ قَبلَ حَتَّى إلَيهِ تَحتاجُونَ ما يَعرفُ
:يَلي كَما صَلُّوا لِذَلِكَ 9 .مِنهُ

‹السَّماءِ في الَّذي أبانا›
،اسْمُكَ لِيَتَقَدَّس
،مَلَكُوتُكَ لِيَأتِ 10
،مَشِيئتُكَ فَتَكُونَ
.السَّماءِ في هِيَ كَما الأرْضِ عَلَى هُنا
،يَومِنا كَفافَ خُبزَنا اليَوْمَ أعطِنا 11
،خَطايانا لَنا وَاغفِرْ 12
.إلَينا يُسِيئُونَ لِلَّذِينَ أيضاً نَحنُ غَفَرْنا كَما
،تَجرُبَةِ في تُدْخِلنا وَلا 13
[a] .الشِّرِّير مِنَ أنقِذْنا بَلْ
،وَالمَجدَ وَالقُدرَةَ المُلْكَ لَكَ لأنَّ
‹آمين .الآبدينَ أبَدِ إلَى

[8] No sean como ellos, porque su Padre ya sabe lo que ustedes necesitan, antes que se lo pidan. [9] Ustedes deben orar así:

»"Padre nuestro que estás en el cielo, santificado sea tu nombre.
[10] Venga tu reino.
Hágase tu voluntad en la tierra, así como se hace en el cielo.
[11] Danos hoy el pan que necesitamos.
[12] Perdónanos el mal que hemos hecho, así como nosotros hemos perdonado a los que nos han hecho mal.
[13] No nos expongas a la tentación, sino líbranos del maligno."

[14] »Porque si ustedes perdonan a otros el mal que les han hecho, su Padre que está en el cielo los perdonará también a ustedes; [15] pero si no perdonan a otros, tampoco su Padre les perdonará a ustedes sus pecados.

THE LORD'S PRAYER IN SPANISH

⁸ Ne les imitez pas, car votre Père sait ce qu'il vous faut, avant que vous le lui demandiez.

(Lc 11.2-4) THE LORD'S PRAYER IN

⁹ Priez donc ainsi: FRENCH
Notre Père,
qui es aux cieux,
que ton nom soit sanctifié[a],
¹⁰ que ton règne vienne,
que ta volonté soit faite,
sur la terre comme au ciel.
¹¹ Donne-nous aujourd'hui
le pain dont nous avons besoin[b],
¹² pardonne-nous nos torts envers toi
comme nous aussi, nous pardonnons
les torts des autres envers nous[c].
¹³ Ne nous expose pas à la tentation[d],
et surtout, délivre-nous du diable[e].
[Car à toi appartiennent
le règne et la puissance
et la gloire à jamais[f].]

¹⁴ En effet, si vous pardonnez aux autres leurs fautes, votre Père céleste vous pardonnera aussi. ¹⁵ Mais si vous ne pardonnez pas aux autres, votre Père ne vous pardonnera pas non plus vos fautes.

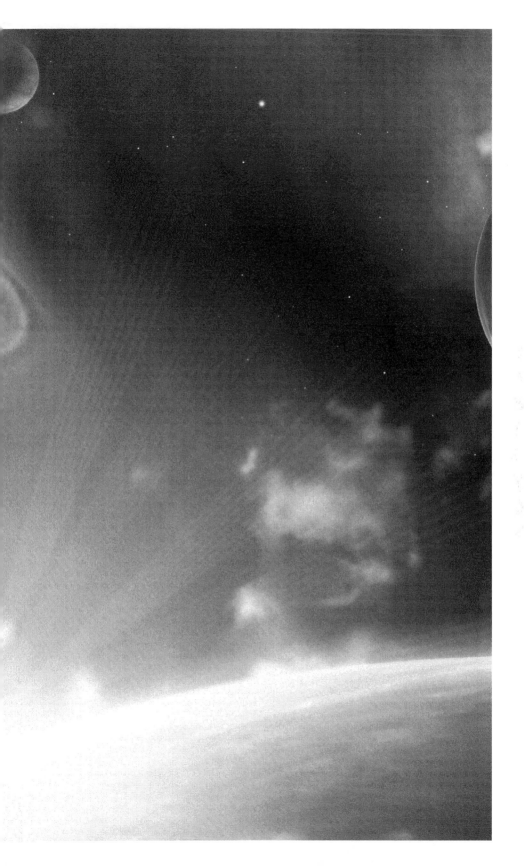

[8] Sidaa darteed ha ahaanina sidooda oo kale, waayo, Aabbihiin waa og yahay waxaad u baahan tihiin intaanad weyddiin. **THE LORD'S**

Tukashaduu Ciise Xertiisii Baray

[9] Haddaba sidatan u tukada, Aabbahayaga jannada ku jirow, magacaagu quduus ha ahaado. [10] Boqortooyadaadu ha timaado, doonistaada dhulka ha lagu yeelo sida jannada loogu yeelo. [11] Kibis maalin nagu filan, maanta na sii. [12] Oo naga cafi qaamahayaga sidaannu u cafinnay kuwa noo qaamaysan. [13] Oo jirrabaadda ha noo kaxayn, laakiin sharka naga du. Waayo, boqortooyada iyo xoogga iyo ammaanta adigaa leh weligaa. Aamiin. **PRAYER IN SOMALI**

[14] Waayo, haddaad dadka u cafidaan xumaantooda, Aabbihiinna jannada ku jira ayaa idin cafiyi doona. [15] Laakiin haddaanad dadka cafiyin, Aabbihiinnu xumaantiinna idiin cafiyi maayo.

THE LORD'S PRAYER IN LUGANDA

8 Kale, temufaanana nga bo: kubanga Kitammwe amanyi bye mwetaaga nga temunnaba kumusaba.

9 Kale, musabenga bwe muti, nti, Kitaffe a1i ggulu, Erinnya lyo litukuzibwe.

10 Obwakabaka bwo bujje. By'oyagala bikolebwe mu nsi, nga bwe bikolebwa mu ggulu.

11 Otuwe leero emmere yaffe eya leero.

12 Otusonyiwe amabanja gaffe, nga naffe bwe tusonyiye abatwewolako.

13 Totutwala mu kukemebwa, naye otulokole eri omubi. Kubanga obwakabaka, n'obuyinza, n'ekitiibwa, bibyo, emirembe n'emirembe, Amiina.

14 Kubanga bwe munaasonyiwanga abantu ebyonoono byabwe, Kitammwe ali mu ggulu anaabasonyiwanga nammwe.

15 Naye bwe mutaasonyiwenga bantu ebyonoono byabwe, ne Kitammwe taasonyiwenga byonoono byammwe.

THE LORD'S PRAYER IN YORUBA

Baba wa ti mbẹ li ọrun

Ki a bọwọ fun orukọ rẹ

Ki Ijọba rẹ de

Ifẹ tire ni ki a ṣe

Bi ti orun, beni li aiye

Fun wa li onje Ojo wa loni

Dari gbese wa ji wa

Bi awa ti ndariji awon onigbese wa

Ma si fa wa sinu idewo

Sugbon gba wa lowo bilisi

Nitori ijo ba ni tire

Ati agbara, Ati ogo

Lailai, Amin

OUR LORD'S PRAYER (IGBO)

West Africa

Nna anyi bi n'igwe
ka aha gi di nso
ka Ala eze gi bia
ka anyi mee ihe i nacho
dika esi ème Ya n'igwe
nye anyi Taa
nke Ga ezuru anyi ubochi taa
gbaghara anyi njor anyi niile
etu anyi si gbaghara ndi meghere anyi
e dubele anyi n'Ime onwunwa
gbaputa anyi n'Aka ajor ihe
n'ihi n'Ala eze bu nke gi
na ike na otuto
Mgbe niile oge niile
Amen

WRITE HERE THE LORD'S
PRAYER
IN YOUR LANGUAGE

The Word 'Believers' in various languages

信徒 In Chinese

Creidsinn in Scottish Gaelic

Gläubige in German

المؤمنين

In Arabic

Creidimh in Irish

מאמינים

In Hebrew

Πιστούς in Greek

信者 in Japanese

Верующие in Russian

Waumini in Swahili

Wierzący in Polish

Troende in Swedish

Onigbagbo in Yoruba

Вірyючi in Ukrahian

مؤمنان

in Persian

Rumaystayaasha in Somali

Creyentes in Spanish

Troende in Danish

Croyants in French

Muminai in Hausa

Amakholwa in Zuru

Abakiriza in Luganda

Müminler in Turkish

kwayan yo in Haiten Creole

ABALOKOLE in Lugunda

The Phrase "The 'born again' Christians" in various languages

ki fèt ankò kretyen yo in Haitian

tekrar doğdu christians in Turkish

waliozaliwa tena wa Kikristo in Swahili

i cristiani di nuovo rinati in Italian

重生的基督徒 in Chinese

ولدوا مسيحيين

In Arabic

los cristianos nacidos de nuevo in Spanish

les chrétiens nés de nouveau in French

рожденные свыше христиане in Russian

os cristãos nascidos de novo in Portuguese

נולד שוב נוצרים

in Hebrew

die wiedergeborenen Christen in German

ndị a mụrụ ọzọ ndị Kraịst in Igbo

de født igjen kristne in Norwegian

οι αναγεννημένοι χριστιανοί in Greek

abazalwa kabusha abangamaKristu
in Zulu

de född igen kristna   in Swedish

na Crìosdaidhean a rugadh a-rithist
in Scottish Gaelic

Become a Partner

Beloved, this ministry of the Written Word by our brother in Christ, requires your participation monetary wise.

This book was made possible through the giving and support of people like you, who desire the best for the people.

Their generosity has made this magnificent work available to the world.

Will you please, start giving to this ministry, please send a gift of support to enable this book and others to go to God lovers.

You may send your seed or monetary gift to:

Bishop Leonard KAYIWA

P.O. Box 1898

Bolingbrook, Illinois 60440

U.S.A.

You can also sow through the secure web site:

www.ministeringtogod.com

www.prayandbelieveGod.org

Bishop's email is:

kayiwaministries@yahoo.com

His wife, Pastor Gail Kayiwa's email is: mrsrev3@gmail.com

God will cause money to multiply back to you when you support this ministry

Normally we tell people to sow a seed of at least $25 in order to get a copy of this book.

We then ship the book to that person immediately.

People have been so gracious towards this mission that they have sown far beyond $25, which has made the shipping of our books easier.

We love you all. You may contact us for prayer. Our phone number is: 224-440-6992

98325262R00163

Made in the USA
Columbia, SC
25 June 2018